VIETNAM

THE WAY IT REALLY WAS

The Patriotism

"I was relieved to go to Vietnam. I wanted to go. I believed it was my duty to serve my country . . . I thought I was one of those macho Mexican Marines who couldn't be hurt."

—*Danny Cruz, Machine Gun Squad Leader, Phu Bai*

The Fighting

"There were guys on top of me in the hole . . . I realized the wet stuff was brain and blood. At first I thought it was mine until I looked above me and saw one guy with the top of his head gone."

—*J.D. Maples, Machinegunner, Firebase Bear Cat*

The Caring

"One night a Marine was brought in, horribly wounded by a grenade. It had blown up in his hands . . . I wanted to comfort him, but there were no hands to hold, no eye to see."

—*Marguerite Giroux, Nurse, Bien Hoa*

VIETNAM: THE HEARTLAND REMEMBERS

STANLEY W. BEESLEY

WE WERE THERE. THIS IS OUR STORY.

STAN BEESLEY
RUDOLPH BRIDGES
WILBERT BROWN
DANNY BRUNER
DAVID CARTER
DANNY CRUZ
MAX DIPPEL
TERRY DYKE
HUGH AND KATHRYN
 FANNING
BOB FORD
MARGUERITE GIROUX

MARK HATFIELD
WILLIE HOMER
JIM HOWARTH
MORRIS JAMES
LEE AND BETSY
 KEYES
ROBERT KIRK
GARY LaBASS
J. D. MAPLES
DAVID MEAD
GREG MOTTO
BILL POFFENBERGER

DAVID PRICE
STEPHEN REDMAN
DAVID SAMPLES
GARY SHERRER
DON SLOAT
NORMAN SUMMERS
BILLY WALKABOUT
JACK WELSH
LES WESTON
MELVIN WREN
JIM YEAROUT

BERKLEY BOOKS, NEW YORK

This Berkley book contains the complete
text of the original hardcover edition.
It has been completely reset in a typeface
designed for easy reading and was printed
from new film.

VIETNAM: The Heartland Remembers

A Berkley Book/published by arrangement with
University of Oklahoma Press

PRINTING HISTORY
University of Oklahoma Press edition published 1987
Berkley edition/March 1989

ISBN: 0-425-11459-7

A BERKLEY BOOK® TM 757,375
Berkley Books are published by The Berkley Publishing Group,
200 Madison Avenue, New York, NY 10016.
The name ''BERKLEY'' and the ''B'' logo
are trademarks belonging to Berkley Publishing Corporation.

PRINTED IN THE UNITED STATES OF AMERICA

10   9   8   7   6   5   4   3   2   1

to
Denise Miles Beesley

Hurrah, boys. We've got them!
—GENERAL GEORGE ARMSTRONG CUSTER
UPON HEARING THAT A LARGE FORCE OF INDIANS
HAD BEEN SIGHTED NEAR THE LITTLE BIGHORN RIVER.

*From earliest times, Oklahoma has played a
vital and often curious role in history.*
—PROFESSOR ARRELL M. GIBSON

*Americans
Just looking around me now,
as we gather here after the mist has cleared
and the crowd has settled
and the noise has ceased
and the bleeding has ended
and the screaming has quieted
and the American dead have been bagged
and the last rounds have stopped flying
and the counting has begun
and the bodies have been piled
and the weapons have been stacked
and there is time to take a deep breath . . .
and just be ourselves. . . .*
—GARY DOBY, OKLAHOMA POET

When you are leaning on your weaker side
To rest the one you wear
This should be a time
Of keen awareness
For any self-appointed cause
Could walk into your lair
This is not a good time to be careless.

Lucas came home a big hero
Though his heart didn't beat, and his eyes
were closed
And, I thought of our childhood games in the
Yard
Playing G.I. Joe.

—MICHAEL RAY LITTLE, TULSA SONGWRITER

CONTENTS

PART THREE
The Edge of the World

PART FOUR
Getting Home

PREFACE

.

The beginning of this project coincided with the heightening of interest in the Vietnam War as a media attraction. America was ready to hear from her sons and daughters fifteen to twenty years after they had fought the war.

Now. Now, America wanted to know.

"Tell us about Vietnam, please," people said. "What was it really like?"

"What went wrong?"

"We are ready to hear about Khe Sanh, Highway 1, Tet, Hamburger Hill, the invasion of Cambodia. Will you tell us?"

The government, Hollywood, Wall Street, the universities, the generals, the politicians, television, radio, journalists, and historians responded: movies, books, journals, documentaries, radio talk shows, histories. Seminars were held on college campuses, parades and rededication ceremonies were scheduled. Mediasponsored GI reunions were put together. The time was right to learn about Vietnam. In the sense of timing, *Vietnam: The Heartland Remembers* capitalizes on this Vietnam vogue.

We hope that our effort is significantly distinctive because of the sovereignty from which we stake our claim to tell of Vietnam: We were there.

Paradoxically, I began this project at a time when I was weary of the subject, having written for five years on personal experiences in the war. I had spoken at schools and colleges about the war. I had written articles. Taught classes. What I had to say about Vietnam had been said at a time when most of America was not listening. And by the time the nation's collective ear had turned, frankly, I believed I could have gone the next five years and been quite content if I never heard the word *Vietnam*.

Circumstances coaxed me out of that feeling. As I reexamined Vietnam again, this time with the rest of America, images too strong for a pen to re-create faithfully marched past my mind and shoved me up, standing: a set of returned bones, a grieving wife and grown family at a belated ceremony, my own baby wearing my tattered beret, a dusty box of letters, a call from a buddy I had almost forgotten but whom I had promised I would never forget.

Images nudged my senses. I saw young, sunburned backs against the lush green jungle. I heard the laughter beneath the boom of big guns. I tasted dirt and warm blood and sweat. I felt again the despair I experienced when I saw my first mangled eighteen-year-old body. I relived the boredom of bunker duty. I felt heat and bone-soaking wetness. I remembered being forced to make profound moral decisions in the time it takes a scissortail flycatcher to snap a bug out of a rotted fence post. I recalled wondering whether I would ever see my Oklahoma home again. I thought about being a very young man.

I realized I would take on the project. No commission appointed me. No governmental agencies nominated me. No organizations asked me to represent them. No foundations financed the project. No groups bankrolled the book.

Vietnam: The Heartland Remembers provides a voice

for the hearts and souls of a body of Oklahomans who fought the Vietnam War. These are their stories in their own words.

We do not claim to represent the thousands of other Oklahomans who served in Vietnam, although we believe we are representative. The deepest regret is in knowing we could not tell the story of every Oklahoman who served in the war. I have spent considerable time in wondering what compelling and fitting story was left out.

No single political bent is represented within. I resisted attempts to flavor the book with dogma. Among our ranks are superpatriots, reluctant warriors, gung-ho marines, skeptics, embittered former patriots, and humanists. Initially, in order to represent another segment of the Oklahoma experience with the war, I had planned to include a draft dodger, but I couldn't find the heart for it. Not in a book from the point of view of those who went.

Ours is an oral history in the spirit of Al Santoli's *Everything We Had* and Mark Baker's *Nam*. We hope *Vietnam: The Heartland Remembers* will do as much to portray the American heartland's experience in Vietnam as the two masterpieces above did of the nation's. The accounts were recorded as autohistory; the narratives were spontaneous. Since much slang and some military terminology was not explained in the text, in an effort not to interrupt the flow of the story, the Glossary was added to define those terms. Some of the language of the book is rough. It is hoped that the reader will be tolerant of our attempt to maintain the accuracy and authenticity of the individual accounts even at the risk of shocking some people.

This is not meant to be a finely tuned journalistic effort or scholarly text. These men and women tell their stories in starts and stops, spurts and hitches. Memories long deadened or shelved are brought to life and taken down to be tested, given air tentatively, and then, with trust established, they gain stride and certainty.

As I began—up the turnpikes and over the gravel roads—I braced myself for negative reaction, for setbacks. I dreaded many of the interviews. I wondered about doors being slammed in my face, telephones being slammed down in my ear. I wondered about interjecting myself and Vietnam into the lives of families who had done with the subject and wanted it left alone. I thought about the pain of tough memories my questions would bring up. I worried about children and how they looked at their daddies and whether what I was visiting about would change any of that.

Upon completing my journey, I realized that most of my fears were not worth worrying about. Oklahomans who went to Vietnam are OK, thank you. Most of them. They are scarred, but tough. They went to Vietnam without a whimper and returned without whining.

Oklahomans do not have to look to Hollywood or Washington, D.C., for heroes. We have them right here at home, walking the streets of Okeene, Snow, Oklahoma City, Tulsa, Durant, Tuttle, Weatherford, Coweta—almost every town, large and small, in the state.

These are men and women who do not think of themselves as heroes; they think of themselves as common folks. Well, they are right. Common men and women thrust by politics and fate into uncommon situations. That is war. That is the Oklahoma experience in Vietnam.

STANLEY W. BEESLEY

Shawnee, Oklahoma

ALONG THE WAY

This project received help and encouragement from Oklahomans in all parts of the state, from the Panhandle to the Pushmataha, from the Cooksons to the Wichitas, from the Cimarron to the Red, from Tulsa to Oklahoma City, from Slapout to Snow:

The wives and families of vets to whom I was a stranger, yet who invited me in, hoping I could be trusted. Betsy Keyes, who so wisely and simply identified this project as a pilgrimage. Kathryn Fanning, whose innocent statement to me in the summer of '84, only days before anyone could know that the remains of her MIA husband would be coming home after fifteen years, that "someone ought to write something about Oklahoma Vietnam veterans, and it should be you," was an element of the genesis of this book.

Friend Larry Battaglia, who expressed concern and who astounded me with the question "Do you think you are up to carrying these people's hearts around in your hands?" The overworked and unsung heroes of the Tulsa Vet Center. The VFW and DAV chapters throughout the state that opened their doors to me. Fellow Ranger Gene Gower, who helped with transportation and nourishment.

Representative Robert Henry, who helped me reach people I had not been able to find. Greg Martin, who told me of others. Ken Leone, who helped on the road. Tag and Spider and Ed, each of whom, in his own way, said, "Go for it."

Richard Carlson and Brad Walck, who read manuscripts and listened to hours of tapes.

My daughters, who put up with Daddy's long hours on the road and at the desk.

My wife, especially, who encouraged, sacrificed, edited, typed, listened, soothed, cajoled, nourished, and otherwise kept me going.

David Samples, Robert Kirk, and Terry Dyke, who, each through his own images, knew exactly why the story should be told.

The principals of the book, those veterans who opened up their souls and trusted me, who let me carry their hearts around in my hands for a short while.

And the thousands of Oklahoma Vietnam veterans whose stories could not be a part of this book but whose spirit is with us.

To all I have mentioned here I say, "Thank you."

S.W.B.

PART ONE

A Sense of Duty

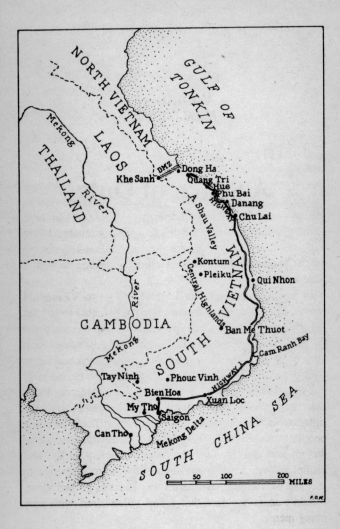

Volunteer

Gary Sherrer
Snow . . . Chu Lai, 1970–71
Medic, Americal Division

I used to walk up to my dad's store in Snow and read in the newspaper what was brewing in Vietnam. In high school I believed what I was reading about Vietnam. I kept track of the enemy body count the government was putting out. It looked like we were winning according to that. I believed it.

In basic I put down that I wanted to go to Vietnam. I wanted to be supportive of my country. I wanted to go, but they sent me to Germany. I remember those cold, bitter German nights when I would sit on the ambulance and look up at the stars and think about guys I knew serving in Vietnam. Why should I be here? It weighed on me heavily.

I requested a transfer. To Vietnam. I volunteered. I was scared about going, but I didn't have any doubts about the rightness of my decision. This might be difficult for some people to understand. This was at a time when morale in the military was down. The war was going badly, and discipline was hard to maintain. Men were desperate to stay out of Vietnam, and here I was eager to go and serve. I didn't share the fact that I had volunteered with very many men.

On my leave home I didn't tell Mom and Dad about my

decision. I just let them assume I had been ordered to the war. But Dad and I were at a game in Kansas City and he turned to me and said, "You volunteered, didn't you?"

The impact my going to Vietnam had on my folks became evident to me on that leave in a very telling way. My dad had always worked very, very hard at the store, with long hours, taking very little time off. But in those days I had left at home he spent a lot of time with me. He took off work, and we went fishing. This was serious business.

When I came back from Vietnam, I was shocked at the way my mom's face had aged. I had traveled first to Denver to spend a couple of days with my sister before coming home. Well, my mother couldn't wait so she came up to Denver. It really got to me when I saw her face. The war had been rough on her.

I learned that my parents had followed the progress of the war closely. They had listened to every report. Once a rocket had hit the base, killing five medics, and of course this upset my parents.

I am proud I served. I didn't care about the statements out, such as "We shouldn't have been there." I was happy to say I went to Vietnam. It had nothing to do with politics.

Of course I saw things that disheartened me. The country boy from Snow, Oklahoma, saw a view of the world that disappointed him. I saw racial tensions that I don't know if I'm over yet. There was a Christmas Eve race riot in our unit. That hurt me very deeply. In my mind I wrestled with the Calley thing. That bothered me. Of course I don't condone what he and others who committed atrocities did, but after being in Vietnam I can understand how those things can come about. All that was hard to take. It was tough. But the thing hardest on me, the most disappointing, was finding out for myself that those figures I read in that newspaper at my dad's store were not true. It was very hard on me when I realized we had really lost.

Seeking the Truth, Passing the Test

Danny Cruz
Tulsa . . . Phu Bai, 1967–68
Machine Gun Squad Leader, Twenty-sixth Marines

As a young man I played football and I boxed. I knew I wanted to go into a branch of the service that was physically demanding. I chose the marines because I wanted to test myself. I think a young man should test himself. It is a good reference point. You'll never know if you can run the race until you're out there on the track.

The Marine Corps to me was a satisfaction, but it wasn't like the John Wayne movies. It was much more demanding. One thing the marines taught me was that a man can go much farther than he thinks he can. You go out for a walk, and if you are by yourself you may stop if you get tired. In the marines you get tired and you will find yourself running. It is a test. I believe I passed it.

I was relieved to go to Vietnam. I wanted to go. I believed it was my duty to serve my country. I knew joining the Marine Corps was the manifestation of that responsibility. It was soon that I realized my experience had to be measured against a two-part truth. Half of it was joining the Marine Corps, and the other part was being in combat. I wanted to see the complete truth.

I wasn't in Vietnam very long. I was only in-country two months before I was hit. I was in long enough to be shot and see several people die beside me. I was there long enough to spend eight months in the hospital.

My Marine Corps training served me well. Even in the confusion of a firefight I reacted in the correct way, the way I had been trained. We got into contact with the NVA thirty feet from us. There is this firing position—I can't even remember now what the marines called it—but it's where you kneel down and support your weapon on your knee. Almost instinctively, in a firefight I assumed this position immediately.

We were on a search-and-destroy mission in the Phu Bai area. Just moving through the country, sweeping. Enemy artillery came in behind us. Our first reaction was to run forward, and that's what they wanted us to do. They had set up an ambush in front of us and they fired artillery behind us. When they fired behind us, we ran right into them.

Unless you've been there, you haven't seen it. I'm not sure what hell is all about, but I know it would resemble a firefight. A fellow marine came running back hit with our own napalm. His utility jacket was burned off him. He knelt down in front of me, and I told him I would take care of him. His whole body was smoking. All the skin of his back was peeled off. The next thing I remember about this man, I asked the corpsman about him and he shook his head, so I knew he'd died. Another marine came running back, his hands covering his face, blood everywhere. He yelled, "My God, I've been shot in the face!" You could see where the bullet had gone through the right eye. He was a young guy, nineteen, blond hair. I told him I'd take care of him and he lay down beside me, his head on his arm. I yelled back at the lieutenant, could we get him out of here? and the lieutenant shook his head no because we were under such a heavy attack there was no way. After a while this boy kicked, and when he kicked the blood gushed out of his eye and he died. I had told both of these men I would take care of them, but what could I do?

I was trying to fire at the enemy. I was one of the first to see them. I saw two gooks pop their heads up. They had utility jackets on and they were well camouflaged. I got up and fired on the offhand position and the lieutenant yelled, "Don't fire at those men, Cruz, they're marines!" I said, "No, sir, those are gooks." They didn't have on helmets and they were well camouflaged, and I knew marines wouldn't take the time to camouflage the way these guys did.

The feeling. I remember the feeling. It was like someone took a sledgehammer or a baseball bat and hit me as hard as he could on the ankle. Then I knew I'd been shot. I thought, like most people, I guess, this can't be happening to me. I thought I was one of those macho Mexican marines who couldn't be hurt. After that, in the hospital, it was like I didn't want to play anymore. Y'know, if you've ever been knocked down in a fight, it's time to sit back, and that's how I felt. I wanted to survive.

The only time I was really afraid was when I was in the hospital in Japan. I wanted to come home. I'd been in there so long. Eight months. One day I asked the doctor what was going to happen to me. He said, "You're going back to the bush." I had sat up when I asked, and I remember laying back down on my rack and thinking, I

am going to die. I knew if I went back to the bush I would
die.

Tent Days

Marguerite Giroux
Oklahoma City . . . Bien Hoa, 1965–66
Nurse, Third Surgical Hospital

Have you ever cared for a seriously wounded young person lying on a canvas cot on the ground? Do you know
how to do it? You do it on your knees. I fed them on my
knees, I treated their wounds on my knees, I held them
and I prayed for God to help them and to help me care for
them—on my knees.

Our hospital, the Third Surgical, was in the perimeter of
Bien Hoa Air Base and consisted of tents with huge red
crosses on top. Only the OR and post-op had wooden
floors; everything else was on the ground on dirt floors,
either dry and dusty or wet and muddy during the monsoon
season. Water brought in by truck. We had old field
equipment and it was primitive. People are shocked to
hear, but in the beginning of the war, when I was there,
the medical facilities in the field were primitive; it seemed
as bad as the Civil War. Medical supplies had no priority
over ammunition, and our unit scrounged to get desper-
ately needed supplies. It seems ridiculous that our army
hospital was in tents when nearby was a huge air base with
an officers' club and swimming pool and all the air force

personnel living in buildings—yet our hospital was housed in tents.

My birthday, October 13, 1965, was the worst day of my life. In one of the first offensive operations in the war, the 173rd Airborne took heavy casualties. Wounded filled our beds and lay all over the ground, literally on the ground. There were so many of them and so little space to put them. They were on wooden cots and rubber mattresses —no pillows. In the surgical tent we had three OR tables separated by sheets. We had to have air and light, so the sides of the tent were rolled up. One-hundred-degree heat and flies don't make for the best aseptic conditions.

I remember a scene that took place in the OR especially vividly because there was a news correspondent doing a story on dust-off for *Reader's Digest.* He watched in amazement as a doctor and nurse got into an argument over a pair of scissors. When you are short of equipment, everyone is tense. You learn to improvise very quickly.

During a push we were worn out. We worked eighteen hours and when we finally had a chance to get some rest, it was next to impossible to sleep with all the noise and the awful heat. During the day jet planes were taking off and landing, trucks rolled by, and helicopters came and went. At night there was artillery and occasional small-arms fire.

The latrines were next to our tent. They didn't want us to wander out at night, but they were too close—the smell was obnoxious. We lived in tents for four months, but we had one luxury over the others. Our CO had scrounged some single beds, actual beds, for the females. That was our big surprise the night we got there in the pouring rain. We raised the tent flaps and there they were, beds in the mud.

Since water was so hard to come by, we had box-stall showers with tarpaulin curtains, and rusty water came from a huge drum on top. We had no laundry facility, so the laundry was taken into Saigon. We had these huge pails, garbage cans actually, you know, that we soaked the linen in. The corpsmen would have to rinse the linen from OR. I'll never forget those poor guys rinsing out the blood clots and pieces of flesh.

There was an Australian unit nearby, and they were very kind to us. We cared for their wounded also, and they would come over and carry litters and help during bad times. When we first arrived, they were extremely upset that the nurses were in such a dangerous area. They took us to a firing range to practice firing our carbines. Yes, we were issued weapons and were glad to have them. I kept mine at the head of my bed.

During lulls we had time off and we were allowed to go to Saigon. We always went in pairs and traveled in fatigues. We were told to change to civilian clothes in Saigon. I learned later this was an attempt to minimize the American presence so the people wouldn't be so aware of the number of military personnel in-country. We didn't think of the danger of traveling the roads at the time. We had the roads by day, and the enemy had them by night. It was always good to get away for a change. We needed it.

Gradually, the tents were replaced by wooden buildings with screened windows and concrete-slab floors. The completion of each building—OR, ward, mess hall, and quarters—was a cause for us to celebrate. Conditions improved and there was more equipment, so more hospitals were opening and the most serious cases were brought to the evac hospitals. Our mission changed, and when the Third Surg was moved to another area, I was transferred to Qui Nhon to the Eighty-fifth Evac Hospital.

At the Eighty-fifth conditions were better. Surgery was housed in a Quonset hut with window air conditioners. We had specialists of every kind: ENT, GU, ortho, and three neurosurgeons. We got the head wounds from all the northern area. I found it difficult to work on these cases; some seemed so helpless.

One night in the holding area I remember a patient screened off from the others. He had an inoperable head wound and was dying. I kept looking in on him whenever I went to call for another case for the OR. He was unconscious. His mom and dad wouldn't know what had happened to him. He was just a boy who probably never even made himself a peanut-butter sandwich, and now he was dying so far from home, and so alone. I wanted to sit with him, but I was too busy; everyone was busy.

Finally our replacements came and it was time to go home. Our time was completed, but we were afraid to go, afraid they couldn't do this job. They were so shocked, so agitated, so dismayed by the wounds—where do you start? I recall a new surgeon pacing back and forth in the OR he was so distressed by it all. Then I remembered: That's how we started. We made it, and they would too.

A Sense of Duty

Norman Summers
Sallisaw . . . Chu Lai, 1969–70
Infantryman, Americal Division

My father was a combat engineer in Italy, was wounded twice, and received a Purple Heart. My father's brother was killed in the line of duty in Europe, and I was named after him. My dead uncle's best friend in the service, Bob Riddle, returned home and married my aunt, my dad's sister. My mother worked in an ammunition factory during the war. My whole family accepted the sacrifices they had to make because they were convinced it was the right cause, as it was.

The only housing I ever remember was GI housing. First in small multifamily apartments in south Sapulpa. When I was five, our family moved to recently built GI tract housing in north Tulsa. All of our neighbors were veterans, most of whom had just started the postwar baby boom. I lived in this house until I went into the army.

I vividly remember my friends' fathers talking about their service experiences, mostly in a positive manner with underlying tones that they had met their, and their country's, sense of duty. I watched *To Hell and Back,* all the John Wayne war movies. I watched *Victory at Sea.* I knew something about the Reds and their worldwide expansion plans.

While I was at Will Rogers High School, my football coach was my main role model. As a high school graduate he had joined the marines and had fought in the major battles of the Pacific. His name was Chuck Boyles. He often spoke with feeling about his experiences. He would speak to us before a game, and often he would relate the concepts of duty, dedication, teamwork, fellowship, and united effort to his war experience. I will say they are still the most motivating presentations I have experienced personally. I saw Coach Boyles recently, and he still talks emotionally about his military service.

During high school I was aware that something was happening in a place called Vietnam, but I wasn't sure if we were supporting the north or the south.

I entered college, primarily in pursuit of the good life. After two semesters in the fun lane, I didn't have a high enough gradepoint average to keep me out of the radically increasing draft. But all I had to do was take this test that summer. If I scored high enough on that test I could keep my 2-S deferment. Well, I somehow missed this test because I was having too much fun the night before. Boy was I in a mess now. It wasn't that I didn't want to serve; when you look at my developmental influences, my role models, and my conditioning, there was no doubt that I was instilled consciously and subconsciously with a sense of duty. But I wanted to continue the good life, and besides, our boys would be kicking ass on those guys soon enough.

I tried the National Guard, but that didn't work out. By June, 1968, my situation was not promising. I had missed quite a few Guard meetings, and they were threatening to activate me. I had lost my job because I was missing too much work. I was drinking much more than I had two months before. My mom and sisters and friends were disappointed with me, and my girlfriend had dumped me because, of all things, I appeared irresponsible. Sounds like the makings of a great country and western song, but it was my life.

I was activated by the Guard. I didn't want to go to Nam, but if that's where they sent me, I wouldn't think twice. My orders were for Germany. I was assigned to a motor company, and I met a lot of Vietnam vets who were serving out their time in Germany.

Money problems were cropping up back home. Everything I made went back home to pay my own bills. I had nothing left over for anything enjoyable. I made a command decision: I would request a 1049, a transfer, to Nam; get combat pay; make rank; apply for an early out; and fight the good cause. Was it a mercenary act? Was it irrational thought process? Was it a sense of duty? Everybody in my company told me I was crazy. A good friend, Steve Fhurmann, showed me a copy of *Stars and Stripes* listing all the men killed that week in Nam. It was a bunch. Sergeant John Gravato, a Nam vet, told me some of his experiences, which were not pretty. But I had done it and that was that.

We flew out of Seattle-Tacoma Airport in September, 1969, to Anchorage, Tokyo, and then into Cam Ranh Bay, Republic of South Vietnam. I had my game face on and expected explosions on the runway as we landed. I was pissed when I was not issued an M-16 as I left the airplane. I was totally stunned when they didn't give me an M-16 when I got to the replacement battalion. Two days later, when they put me on a plane headed for Chu Lai without a weapon, I was scared. The plane had three short stops before Chu Lai, and I expected to be fired on at every stop.

I viewed Vietnam from the air, and it was beautiful. The

lushest, densest greens I have ever seen. But even the scenery could not calm my anxiety.

They finally gave me a weapon when I got to my company area. Along with a steel pot, rucksack, ammunition, and poncho liner. I rode out to LZ Professional with an eighteen-year-old kid from Michigan. The LZ was a small hill in the foothills of the mountains on the border between Vietnam and Cambodia. Four companies were at Professional, along with a mortar platoon, a battery of 105 howitzers, a headquarters, an echo recon platoon, and a mess hall. We had helipads, upper and lower, and a perimeter fortified with barbed wire, trip wires, claymores, and bunkers.

The grunts went out on fifteen-day patrols—field trips, we called them—and then would come in for a few days to pull perimeter guard, burn shit, pull KP, check the wire. Part of our AO covered a portion of the Ho Chi Minh Trail. On the patrols we covered everything from ambushes to search and destroy, reconnaissance, sensor placement, and combat assaults.

We were in what was called a free-fire zone. If anybody was seen, we could fire on them without checking with anybody. There was not supposed to be any peasants, farmers, sightseers, or anybody in our area.

My sense of duty and faith in my government's knowledge, intent, and wisdom started to erode. We lost three men in one afternoon. We walked back to the LZ, and I saw their body bags on the helipad; they couldn't be flown out due to the weather. Something in me snapped. This was a turning point in my life, the way I view life. That day I wrote a letter to my congressman, Page Belcher, asking him why we were in Vietnam and was he aware that Americans were doing it all for the South Vietnamese? In our area, not only did we never see any peasants, we never saw any South Vietnamese soldiers, either. We, the Americans, were doing all the work and suffering all the losses. I asked my congressman had he ever seen a friend lay in a body bag treated like so much trash? Representative Belcher's response was a form letter of his family's military service. I don't think I have the mastery of the English language to express my disgust at his response.

By this time my sense of duty was to myself and to my brothers caught up in the same situation. I had about eight months left in-country at this time.

A sense of duty? I definitely have one. It has changed some, but it is still strong. My strongest sense of duty may sound paradoxical. It is to the dead and living. To the dead it is a duty to hold their names high. The fact that they gave their lives in Vietnam is every bit as meaningful as my uncle who gave his life in World War II. It is a duty not to allow anything to diminish their courage.

My duty to the living is to evaluate what our government says and does in the hope that we will not make the tragic mistakes of Vietnam again. I personally feel that it is the duty of all of us to evaluate what our government does and let our opinions be known. I also feel a duty to the men who made it through the Nam but are still prisoners of their memories and experiences. When I get depressed or involved with what appears to be a great problem, I remember what tough was, what Vietnam was, and the many men who don't have the opportunity to get themselves involved in the petty problems we blow out of proportion. They are buried and have their names on a wall in the capital. I realize how fragile life is.

Black Marine

Rudolph Bridges
Muskogee . . . Dong Ha, 1967–68
Fire Direct Controlman, Third Marine Division

Lots of black guys went to the Nam and came back thinking somehow it was gonna be different here in the States. Then they found out nothing had changed, and it made them bitter.

When first back, I flew into Dallas. I had on my uniform with my medals, feeling good about myself. Proud, too. I'd done something. I had served thirteen months in Vietnam for my country. I don't know, maybe I was looking for special treatment. I go to this restaurant, and I sit down. I sat and sat and sat. A long time. Finally a waitress came over, and the look in her eyes was, "What are you doing in here?" It really hurt me. Tears came into my eyes. I had been looking for something that wasn't there.

I knew I would go to Vietnam. I had mixed emotions about it. I was a little gung ho and I was scared, too. I wanted to prove myself, I wanted to test my manhood, but I was very worried about my mother and father. I knew it would be hard on them.

I was very rebellious. Didn't want to take orders from a white man. There was so much prejudice and discrimination in the military that resentment just kept building up on the part of the brothers. We did all we could to hassle the Man, y'know. We would crush our caps and grow beards and not blouse our boots. We did it to irritate.

A lot of what I saw in Nam bothered me. I even began to think atheist from the things I saw happening. Fortunately, later I came to my senses because I do believe in God the Almighty. Most black guys, I think, didn't know what we were fighting for. Some thought there was a war going on back home on the streets. It was tough enough back there, so why did we have to come over here and fight? For the black man, Vietnam became more of a survival thing.

I heard of blacks and whites being real close to each other in the bush. But I know a black kid, a grunt, whose unit was hit bad. A white guy got hit, was hurt bad. And this young brother he risked his life going back in to get him. He carried this white dude out who was hurt bad, and the gooks firing at them, and this guy kept saying, "Put me down, nigger."

We were so close to the DMZ we could watch the little suckers load up on us every day. From January to March, we lived in a hole like rats. We took incoming every day. The rounds hit close. It was funny about whites and blacks then, too. White guys had this John Wayne thing, y'know, like they wanted in the action. They would jump up out of the trenches and on top of the bunkers. Crazy! And get killed, too. No way a brother was going to do something like that. We fought, but we knew how to survive, too. In fact, I think more blacks fought in the field than whites, percentagewise.

Black men got along better with the Vietnamese, I think, because there was an empathy between us. They knew something about what we'd been through. Especially the kids. They looked up to us. Liked our jive talk, and they caught on to the con game a lot of black guys know. I used to stay with the villagers. I'd go off limits into the villages, where we weren't supposed to go. What was they gonna do to me? I was already in Nam. I'd take my weapon with me, but still it was a little crazy, looking back at it. I'd jump off the truck, roll off the road, and hide in the weeds for a little while. I'd sneak into the village and stay for two or three days at a time. I liked the Vietnamese, but I never completely trusted them.

Body Escort

Mark Hatfield
Coweta . . . LZ North English, 1969–70
Paratrooper, 173d Airborne Division

My roster number came up one day out in the field. I didn't have any idea what for. They told me, "Get your stuff ready. You're going back to the rear. There is a bird coming for you." Helicopters, I'll never forget them. I won't for the rest of my life. I don't care what I'm doing, when I hear a helicopter, I stop and look up and watch it till it gets out of sight. If I'm inside, I'll go to a window or walk outside to watch it. I went back to LZ North English, and there they sent me somewhere else. Then I knew what it was for. Nobody told me. I just knew.

Coweta is a little ol' town, but we lost so many in the war. My friends. Don Sloat, Buddy, Jimmy Campbell, Eddie Pulliam, Phillip Sanders, Frankie Faught. Killed in action. There were people in town upset. Y'know, "Coweta has paid her price" and "No more!" and all that. There was talk of pulling all the Coweta boys out of the service. I knew some politicians were working on it. People talked to me about it, but I didn't want to get involved with that.

What they wanted me out of the field for was I was going to take Jimmy Campbell's body home. By now, people back home knew how it worked. They'd seen enough boys come home dead. It hurt when I found out about Jimmy. I didn't want to believe it. It can't be happening again, I thought. After all those others, and now Jimmy.

I think Frankie was the first killed. And the crazy thing, Don bought Frankie's car, an old '57 Chevrolet. Don joked around and said, "Well, I guess I'll be killed too." He kidded around about it, but in a way, I think deep down he really believed it. I took Don's death pretty hard. 'Course we went in together. Don and I volunteered for the draft. We were trying college and we were tired of it; I didn't want to book it and Don didn't want to book it. Vietnam was going on and I thought I ought to do something. I came home one Friday from school and I told Don I was volunteering for the draft. He said, "I'll go with you."

We went down to the draft board and the lady said, "You want to go Wednesday or a month from Wednesday?" I looked at Don, and I told him, "Look, you know if we wait a month we might not want to go." Heck, Wednesday we were on our way.

We took our physicals in Oklahoma City. Don was in the other line laughing his head off. "I flunked the physical," he kept saying. "You lyin' sucker," I said. But no, he really flunked it. High blood pressure. He had to go three times until he passed it. He had his mind made up to go. Don and I were real close. I think his mother wanted me to come home with his body, too, but it didn't work out.

Once they got me cleaned up from the field and in a new uniform, they flew me from Nam to San Francisco, where I was supposed to pick up Jimmy's body. We went to this giant warehouse. There were other men, too, escorting bodies to different places all over the country. Most of them didn't know the guys they were taking home. Y'know, they picked guys from the same place back home, but it could be a big city. 'Course that's not the way it was with me and Jimmy. We stood in this big, cold warehouse with all those bodies in metal caskets. I will never forget it as long as I live. Nobody said a word. It was quiet. We heard the steps of an officer walking toward us in a trench coat. That was the only sound.

I stayed with Jimmy's body. I was supposed to never leave it. They didn't have to tell me that.

A guy loading the plane wasn't going to let the U.S. flags stay on the coffins. I said, "What's it gonna hurt?" He said, "The flags come off." I got to thinking about it and it made me mad. " 'Look,' I said, 'the flags stay on. That's the way it's gonna be.' " I guess he knew I meant it, 'cause he left them on.

Later, when I went back to Vietnam, a lot was made over the letter I wrote to the state representative when they were trying to get me out of Vietnam. I never meant it to be more than what it was: just a letter from one person to another telling him I appreciated what he was trying to do for me, but I felt like I had to stay and do my duty. It got in the papers and made me out to be a hero or something in some people's eyes. That wasn't the way it was. I felt so sorry for what happened to my friends and their families. But it wouldn't be right to take me out just because I was from Coweta. I wouldn't have felt right.

Remembering Hugh, MIA

Kathryn Fanning for Hugh Fanning
Oklahoma City . . . Danang, 1967
Marine Fighter Pilot

Have I wasted most of my adult life loving a man who probably is dead? Most people might think so, but anyone who knew Hugh Fanning understands. I couldn't help loving Hugh when I met him at the University of Dallas, and I can't help loving him now.

For seventeen years I wondered if Hugh was a prisoner, held captive in Southeast Asia, or was killed when his A-6 Intruder crashed October 31, 1967. For eleven months after I buried his purported remains on August 8, 1984, I thought I also could bury the past. When I learned that I was given only partial remains, I had the body exhumed and sought help to identify it. I asked two certified anthropologists to evaluate the identification made by the Central Identification Laboratory in Hawaii. The results? Neither anthropologist could positively identify the bones as belonging to my husband.

And so the waiting continues, this time with new images.

Those thirty pieces of medium-gray bone remain locked up in the state medical examiner's laboratory while I try to find, search for, X-rays taken of my husband while he was in the Marine Corps. Every day I wonder if the bones did indeed belong to Hugh or if they belonged to someone else's loved one.

I prefer to think of Hugh as he was when I last saw him: ramrod straight in a khaki uniform with perfect creases.

When I first met Hugh, I'd never imagined that he would show an interest in a uniform, much less perfect creases. A couple of my friends and I used to station ourselves in a student-union window at the University of Dallas, betting on when Hugh would appear, sleepy eyed, from his dormitory. We also bet on how many days in a row he would wear a certain gray crew-necked sweater with holes in one shoulder. Twelve days was his record. I was smart enough not to put money on the thirteenth day.

We weren't the only women who watched Hugh. He was considered extremely popular, along with his roommate, Richard Francis Kelly. Those two could make any dull gathering spring to life when they walked into the room. They had a combination of intelligence and wit. Neither was the straight man in his comedy routines.

At first I laughed at my female classmates when they vied for Hugh's attention. I appreciated his humor, but I thought his British accent was strange. I learned that he'd attended school in England as well as Italy and Germany. His father worked for Radio Free Europe. I became fascinated watching Hugh clown around in the cafeteria, confusing his friends by speaking in different languages. It didn't seem to matter that he had overslept through his morning classes. He maintained an honors average while editing the school newspaper and playing roles in our college productions.

I think I fell in love with him when he played the part of the fireman in *The Bald Soprano*. He was apple cheeked with makeup. He wore a red lumberjack shirt and a fire chief's helmet.

I was glad that Hugh had awful hair. Wiry, the color of a mongrel. It kept him from being too perfect. He couldn't afford haircuts. Twiglets of hair would reach his collar before some sympathetic female would whip out her scissors and save him.

Hugh's eyes, on the other hand, were beautiful. Cornflower blue. They tilted up at the corners, like a cat's. When Hugh smiled, his eyes looked mischievous. When he didn't, they looked wistful. His eyes didn't seem to go with the bottom half of his face. I couldn't decide if he was good looking or not until I fell in love with him. Then I knew he was gorgeous.

Maybe it was inevitable that our attraction would be as sure as metal filings to a magnet. Both of us were used to lots of attention, whether we wanted it or not. In fact, my relationship with Hugh was the one thing that makes me consider the possibility of predestination.

Silly clues foreshadowed our marriage, though we didn't recognize them until later. I was dating Hugh's roommate, Rich, when I was faced with a term paper deadline. Though Rich was as intelligent as Hugh, for some reason I turned to Hugh for help. Hugh looked at my table piled high with books, notes on index cards, and crumpled false starts. Then he gave me his lopsided smile. In a matter of minutes he scanned my material and wrote an easy-to-follow outline. I was impressed, so impressed with his ability to organize that I scribbled a note, "I, Hugh Fanning, promise to marry Sylvia Kathryn Price," and shoved it toward him for his signature. He didn't hesitate. He signed it. I kept the note, though within days I left for Christmas vacation. I returned from break wearing an engagement ring from my high school sweetheart.

Later, I learned that someone, probably surprised that I traded Rich Kelly for my high school boyfriend, told Hugh, "That crazy Sylvia came back engaged." Hugh, I was told, shrugged it off with, "She won't marry him. She's going to marry me." I laughed about Hugh's not wanting to "move in on his roommate's territory" but having no regard for the competition of my high school sweetheart.

From then on, Hugh seemed to be everywhere I was. I became captivated by his knowledge of history, art, Europe. I had led a sheltered childhood on an Oklahoma dairy farm, and though my parents had a city background and an extensive education, I was in awe of the way Hugh had lived. I might as well have been the stereotypical country girl with little book larnin', the contrast was so great next to Hugh's sophistication. It seemed to me that Hugh must know everything there was to know. One evening while I savored Hugh's words, a classmate dashed in with the message that my fiancé was on the telephone long distance. I was annoyed. I went back to the dorm to take the call. Halfway there, it occurred to me that I wasn't ready to get married, at least not to my high school sweetheart. Hugh was much more interesting.

The next day I carefully wrapped my diamond ring and mailed it back to Oklahoma City. I can't remember exactly when Hugh asked me to marry him, but somehow it was understood. Our friend, Father Breedlove, Hugh's dorm supervisor, called it a marriage made in heaven.

Ironically, I agreed to marry Hugh to keep him from joining the Marine Corps. After graduation, his roommate, Rich, had joined, and Hugh said he would, too, if we didn't get married. Somehow I knew that if Hugh went off to the service, I'd never see him again.

Amused by superstition, we chose Friday, the thirteenth of September, 1963, as our wedding day. We didn't bother to invite anyone outside the immediate family to the wedding. We were surprised when the church filled up with friends who had learned of our plans.

It was a mediocre wedding, unfit for the pages of *Bride* magazine. I wore a cream-colored sack dress with a drawstring waist. Hugh bought me a wedding bouquet, since my parents had more children than money. We ate a ghastly fish dinner at the Holiday Inn afterwards. Those were the days when Catholics didn't eat meat on Fridays. I would have killed for a peanut-butter sandwich. Instead, I settled for a basket of buttered rolls. I regretted our decision to marry on that particular day of the week.

I wasn't in a hurry to drive back to Fort Worth for our wedding night. Hugh and I had found a place in the Lucerne Apartments: a living room with a Murphy bed that swung down from a closet and a kitchen the size of a handkerchief. In fact, Hugh got testy when I insisted on staying late with my cousins, Father Denis and Father Morris. I'd loved them since childhood. Hugh and I scarcely spoke on the trip home.

Like most women who had saved themselves for their husbands, I was reluctant to leave the safety of our bedroom. My mother had given me a yellow nylon nightgown. It evoked a response from Hugh that didn't brighten the evening. He looked at the limp fabric dotted with appliqué of beige lace and muttered, ''You've got to be kidding.'' I always blamed my mother for sabotaging my wedding night. I suppose she was intent on my remaining a virgin.

I took my duties as a wife too seriously. I made home-made bread and desserts every day until Hugh complained that he was gaining weight. I was so used to cooking for my four brothers and parents that I had a hard time cooking for just two. Hugh put on twenty pounds before he sentenced me to fixing lean hamburger patties and salads only.

His temporary pudginess led him into a new phase in his life: running. He bought us matching gray sweatsuits and told me that we were going to jog every day. I was as enthusiastic about the idea of exercise as I had been about arithmetic class when I was in grade school. When I discovered I was pregnant, I lied to Hugh, telling him that my doctor said I couldn't run anymore. He allowed me to sit on a park bench while he raced around the track, again and again, until his cheeks were the color of a stop sign. To impress me with his workout, Hugh would strip off his sweatshirt and wring it out, making trails of water onto the dirt at my feet.

Physical fitness became an obsession with Hugh, and he began to play handball and work out with weights. He used to insist that I ask, "Which way to the beach?" so he could put his elbow out and point to show his bulging biceps. I teased him for preening in front of the mirror. "You love yourself enough for both of us," I told him. He agreed.

That first year of our marriage, Hugh taught math at Trinity Valley Boys School in Fort Worth. Though he admired the headmaster, he hated teaching.

About a month before our first baby was due, the subject of the Marine Corps came up again.

"What do you think?" Hugh asked me.

"You'll get killed in Vietnam," I answered. I know I gave him a sullen look.

He laughed. "Why are you such a fatalist?"

I knew better than to argue. Besides, my mother had trained me to be totally obedient to my husband. "A woman should wait on a man hand and foot," she told me again and again. "A man is the head of the house."

Ironically, after all of his talk about the Marine Corps, Hugh first went to an Air Force recruiter. I'll always wonder if Hugh would be alive today had the recruiter been better. As it was, he quoted Hugh the base pay of an officer without mentioning any of the other benefits, such as separation allowance, combat pay, and so on. Hugh was discouraged. He knew he couldn't support a wife and child on the meager amount. Hugh went to the Marine Corps recruiter, who made sure Hugh knew all of the service benefits. He joined.

I agreed to stay with Hugh's parents in New York while he was in officer candidate school in Quantico, Virginia. It was uncomfortable with my in-laws. No one in the family expressed any affection with the others. I was used to a hug-me, kiss-me family which ran out into the front yard to greet my father when he got home from work. At the Fannings', no one bothered to look up from homework when my father-in-law came home. I was astonished that my mother-in-law refused to do small favors, such as heat the milk for her husband's coffee, when my own mother had drummed waiting on a man into my attitude.

I was almost at the point where I couldn't stand the situation anymore when I broke my back in an automobile accident and was hospitalized for several months. I was taken to Grasslands County Hospital and later transferred to St. Alban's Naval Hospital when I was able to be moved from a Stryker frame into a body cast. The pain in my back was searing, but it was nothing compared to my missing our baby, Kelly.

Once when Hugh was on leave he smuggled Kelly into

my room in a brown grocery sack. I was astonished to see that her hair had changed color, and she was three times the size she was when I'd last seen her. She had an eye infection that worried me for days until I got word that it had cleared up.

After my body cast was removed, I was told I could join Hugh and Kelly in Florida, where Hugh was in flight training. Since the hospital personnel had cut off my clothing after the accident and Hugh had packed my clothes and taken them to Florida, I hobbled to the hospital BX and bought a sweatshirt and corduroy slacks.

It took me five days on a military air transport to fly from New York to Pensacola. The plane seemed more intent in breaking down than in transporting. The weather was bitterly cold, and I huddled under a military blanket someone else shared.

I was always clever about looking for the proverbial silver lining. I found one in our box lunches. I limped down the aisle of the airplane during its many rests on the ground and asked other passengers if they wanted their Hershey bars. I collected a nice stash that kept me happy in spite of the pain, the cold, and the delays.

They drove me out to the hospital in Pensacola where I was supposed to be admitted for physical therapy. I was told that my medical records had been lost. Again a silver lining. I figured that I wouldn't have to fool with any more hospitals, since no one seemed to know what to do with me. I fumbled in my pocket for the address of the woman who was taking care of Kelly for Hugh. Then I called for a cab.

I had trouble expressing my gratitude to our baby sitter. I had lost the ability to talk to people. I had stayed in the hospital so long. It was the first time in my life that I felt shy and at a loss for words. I asked for directions to our base housing.

Hugh was unable to meet me. He was at a survival school. I was terrified to carry Kelly by myself. She was so heavy and my back was so weak. I managed to bathe her and feed her, then I sank into bed, exhausted.

I was asleep when I heard footsteps in the room. I opened my eyes and saw Hugh standing at the foot of the bed in dirty fatigues. He smiled his funny half-smile, and I reached out for him. I wrinkled my nose at the smell of the camp fires in his uniform. I never wanted to be separated from him again, not for a day.

Hugh seemed so different. His first Marine Corps photograph showed him with round cheeks, looking like a boy dressed up for a school play. Later photographs showed a lean face, tight with determination. Hugh joked about the Marine Corps making him a trained killer, but I didn't consider it amusing. He also used to tell me that if the Marine Corps had wanted him to have a wife, it would have issued him one. I sighed through the ridiculous verses like "This is my pistol, this is my gun; this is for shooting, this is for fun." Hugh always had to explain them to me.

Though I understood the necessity of a pecking order in the military, I had trouble seeing anyone as being above or below anyone else. I was not impressed by the women who wore their husbands' rank and was bored by the endless bridge games. I fell into the pattern of many officers' wives with babies: taking turns making coffeecake with Bisquick and watching one another's children when we had to go to the commissary.

Hugh and I were poorer than the others, since we had college debts to pay. Also, many of the other officers and their wives had allowances from wealthy parents. One wife in particular bothered me by showing me the king-sized fourteen-karat-gold charms on her bracelet and her many sterling-silver goblets. Hugh and I had no furniture except for our bed and the baby's bed. It was only after Hugh had left for Vietnam that I bought our first television set, a mixer, and a toaster.

It was hard to believe that Hugh was the same person who couldn't manage to wake up for his morning classes in college. He annoyed me with his "Rise and shine!" and his insistence that I join him in daily exercise. When I got pregnant with our son, Michael, and our daughter Erin, Hugh didn't believe my old the-doctor-won't-let-me stories anymore. He bought me a copy of *The Royal Canadian Exercise Book* and evaluated my workouts on the charts. I still read his comments occasionally, written in his crimped, left-handed handwriting: "Frappy situps." "Lousy leglifts."

Hugh would frown whenever he examined my 101-pound body for excess fat. He sorted through the wastepaper basket when he got home from work, counting the candy bar wrappers and chiding me for my lack of willpower. "I'm a stoic," he always claimed. "You're just a hedonist."

It was true. My idea of heaven was a six-pack of Fudgesickles or a giant candy bar. Hugh never knew that I made enormous sheet cakes because I would eat exactly half before he got home and then fit the rest into a smaller pan.

Hugh had a compulsion for perfection. This goaded me into frenzies of housecleaning. I never would have believed his newly found love of order in the old days when I sneaked into his dorm room. In college I could unearth enough soft-drink containers from Hugh's piles of dirty clothes to supply a bottling plant. Those days, like his wiry hair, were gone.

I felt lost when Hugh told me he had orders to Vietnam. I couldn't bear the thought of his leaving. Who would make me exercise? Who would put the cap back onto the toothpaste? I tried to kid with him about how things would go to hell in a handbasket, but the truth was, I was terrified.

Hugh must have been afraid, too, but it wasn't his way to show it. I put on my best compliant-wife face, determined not to cry when his plane left in June of 1967. I was surprised that Kelly didn't cry, either. She was three then. She and Hugh had been extremely close; there was a very strong bond there. At the airport on Hugh's day of departure, Kelly was distracted by singer Connie Haines, who had called her over to her seat for a chat. Michael was the only one who cried.

While Hugh was gone, I read and reread all his letters, starting from the very first he wrote while in Quantico:

29 September, 1964

Dear Sylvia,

I arrived in Quantico accompanied by pelting rain, the first the area has had in many weeks. Apparently we have some sort of mystical rapport with the rain gods . . . or is it just me? Did NY clear up after I left?

At any rate, although not much has happened so far, I'm pretty sure this will be as enjoyable a sojourn as would be possible without having you along to share things with.

I'm shorn and adorned with the very best the USMC has to give . . . including red and yellow satin gym shorts!

This morning, we spent some 4½ hours being issued equipment and clothing. It was a maddening experience. No one was familiar with terminology, and the sight of "Dickies, men's" threw me into a quandary when I spotted it on my supply list . . . they turned out to be undershorts.

This afternoon we got Marine Corps haircuts. Any conceivable fondness I ever entertained for short haircuts as becoming to me has been dispelled. It is comfortable though. At any rate, my head looks now like a talented bowling ball.

This getting up at 5 A.M. isn't really bad. The only lousy thing was marching in a downpour to breakfast and equipment issue. Rather than write every day, Syl, why don't we just answer each other's letters. That way no confusion should develop.

I miss you very much, and I love you more. Give my best to everyone. Love especially to Kelly F.

                              Love,
                              HUGH

The high point of every day was the trip down the hallway of our apartment in Alameda, California (Hugh left me on the West Coast to see if I'd like it enough to stay if he got out of the service). I'd unlock the mailbox at the end of the hall, holding my breath until I spotted the familiar red, white, and blue airmail letters, with *free* printed in crimped handwriting where a postage stamp would normally be.

Hugh's letters grew more insistent, since he wanted me to meet him in Hawaii for R&R. I ignored his request that I make airline reservations, though, because something inside me warned that I would never have the chance to meet him.

I could feel the dark days ahead approach as surely as a train on a track. I couldn't tell anyone of my fears since I knew no one to tell. But every day, when I would see a Marine in the apartment complex, something knotted in my solar plexus. Was he the one? Would he be the one to tell me that Hugh was dead?

I tried to tell myself that I was crazy, that my anxieties were nothing unusual. Any wife would worry about her husband's return from Vietnam.

The day before Halloween in 1967 (which was Halloween in Vietnam), our three-year-old daughter Kelly confirmed my unspoken dread.

"Mommy!" Kelly looked up at me from her dinner. Tears streaked her cheeks. "Daddy's hurt."

It felt like cold wrapping its fingers around my neck. I could hardly swallow.

"What do you mean, Daddy's hurt?" was what I managed to whisper.

"His legs. They hurt bad," Kelly told me.

I held her for a long time, rocking back and forth in an effort to console her. I couldn't explain it, but I knew she was telling the truth.

I slept very little that night. Images of Hugh with his funny half-smile invaded my sleep. My head was stuffy from a combination of crying and a severe cold.

The next morning a thundering knock at the apartment door woke me. Go away, I thought, whoever you are. I covered my head with a pillow to drown out the sound. I finally was forced to come out for air since my nose was so stopped up. Go knock on someone else's door, I told the intruder silently. I don't have to answer it if I don't want to.

The knocking wouldn't go away. It became louder, more insistent. I scrambled out of bed. Resigned, I glanced at the bedroom mirror, disgusted at the sight of my face. My hair stood out from my head like spines on a porcupine. My eyes were swollen into pink marshmallows. The skin around my nostrils was red and cracked. You'll be sorry, I thought. I don't need a Halloween mask, whoever you are.

I had on my orange-striped nightshirt. I slipped on a trench coat and cracked open the front door. At last, there they stood. Marines.

"My husband is dead, isn't he?" I asked them, wanting to get their visit over as quickly as possible.

I unfastened the chain and the men stepped inside. The older one looked like Joseph Cotten and the younger, dark-haired man stared at his shoes, like he was examining the shine.

"We're not sure, ma'am," the older one said. He sat on the sofa and unsnapped his briefcase.

They took turns explaining that my husband's plane was shot down over North Vietnam. They said it was doubtful that he could have survived, even if he had managed to eject from his aircraft. His plane was just 450 feet above the ground when it was hit, probably by a surface-to-air missile. I refused to consider their words. I would think about it later, in privacy. I concentrated on the basket of dirty laundry beside the sofa. I would NOT break down in front of them.

Finally, they left. My mouth was soured, like it had the copper taste of death. How could I possibly deal with this? I had promised to take the children trick-or-treating that evening. How could a woman with a dead husband dress up in costume and walk around the block with three babies? It made no sense. I stared at Hugh's picture on the coffee table. My throat tightened as if someone had twisted a rope on my neck.

"You bastard!" I screamed at his picture, "I wouldn't have done it to you!" I felt as if I were watching a movie

of unspeakable horror and I'd always known the ending.
"Come back, damn it, or I'll kill you!" The ludicrousness
of what I'd said made me laugh. I was hysterical. I
laughed until I was limp as a rag doll. I cried until I
couldn't see through the slits that were my eyes. I made
myself struggle into a black Halloween eye mask. At least
the children wouldn't have to see my pain when they woke
up.

That night, I dressed the children and took them around
the block for candy. Kelly was three, Michael two, and
Erin eight months. I felt like a very old woman who had
lived longer than she wanted to.

Night after night I slept lightly, waiting to hear another
knock at the door with news about Hugh. Weeks crawled
by. Months. Years.

Tet In Can Tho

Jack Welsh
Oklahoma City . . . Can Tho, 1967–68
Physician, Volunteer Physicians for Vietnam Program

A few weeks before Tet, 1967, I started working in the
civilian provincial hospital in Can Tho down in the Delta
about one hundred kilometers south of Saigon. I was there
as part of the AMA's Volunteer Physicians for Vietnam
Program (VPVN). Dr. Malcolm Phelps from El Reno was
in-country head of the program and had met us in Saigon.

Dr. Hershel Douglas was his assistant, and they lived in Can Tho. I had known both of them when they were medical students at Oklahoma so it seemed to me the state was well represented in the effort to help the people of the country.

The civilian hospital was an old French building supposedly built in the late 1800s. Most of the Vietnamese physicians were in the military so Americans were taking care of the patients. Obstetrics was done by midwives except for cases requiring surgery. There was an air force surgical team, four other VPVN physicians—two general surgeons, an ophthalmologist, and an orthopedist—and a medical student. They had about 100 to 150 surgery cases a month but even had time to do one mitral-valve repair. For my part I saw between 100 and 125 outpatients, children and adults, a day and took care of three inpatient wards. There was a Vietnamese interpreter who worked with each of us.

Since I was the only internist, I was lucky there was a Special Forces C team at the airport. They had two internists, Dr. Bruce Dunn, stationed there, and a Walter Reed team member, Dr. Ed Colwell, who was in town part of the time. They came over and helped whenever they could and were an immense help. Patients came from all over the delta, and occasionally a group came down the Mekong from Cambodia to be seen.

Two of the wards were general-medicine wards with a total of about sixty to seventy beds. The other service was a so-called intensive-care ward with about eighteen beds, but frequently it would have one or two additional carriers with patients. In this ward children and adults were mixed, and there were usually two to three patients in half the beds. The patients' families stayed on the ward and helped take care of the patients and supplemented the two meals a day of rice and fish with food they cooked on the hospital grounds. At night they slept on the floor of the ward and under the beds.

The family units were very close, with parents taking care of their children and children taking care of their elderly parents. They were very appreciative of everything we tried to do. They accepted their diseases in a very stoic manner. None wanted to die in the hospital. If the family thought the patient was terminal, they took him home to die.

There were no facilities for isolation, and patients with two different highly contagious diseases were frequently in the same bed. The common diseases were ones we no longer see in the United States. It was not unusual for a patient to come to the clinic for some other medical problem and show the early signs of leprosy. Diphtheria, typhoid, amoebic colitis, amoebic abscesses of the liver, malaria, cerebral malaria, emphysema, ascariasis, and tetanus were seen almost every day. The killer among the infants was diarrhea, as it is in all Third World countries.

The government's vaccination program had worked and there were no smallpox patients. There was an epidemic of cholera and I had over sixty cases. The hospital had old cholera cots with a hole cut in the middle so the patient could have diarrhea in his bed, and you could put a big pan underneath it for collection of the liquid stool. Thanks to the good supply system that Dr. Douglas had established, we had plenty of fluids and only lost one patient. It wasn't possible with the limited facilities to make a diagnosis in every case; however, we had to fill out a chart and a fact sheet with a diagnosis each time, which was sent to Saigon for their statistics. I often wondered what they did with our diagnosis. BORK (Buddha Only Really Knows).

Can Tho was fairly quiet in 1967. There were occasional rockets, fired into the town at night, and the airport came under attack a few times, but there was not a lot of evidence of the war except for civilian casualties brought into the hospital. The people were wonderful, and Tet was beautiful. The market on the river was always full of food and fish for sale, but at Tet there was even more produce and lots and lots of flowers. Everything was cleaned up and repainted to start the New Year.

I was put on call the night before Tet, since the surgeons thought there wouldn't be any casualties and they had planned a party. Just before sunset a ten-year-old girl was brought in who had been shot. She had been standing right in front of the hospital and the bullet had come almost straight down and had gotten a clavicle and nicked the lung. There had been the usual firing in the distance, but nothing close, so I couldn't figure out how it had happened. I then found out from my interpreter and the other hospital people that at Tet everyone shot off firecrackers and those with weapons would fire live ammunition in the air. After calling out the surgical team—since there were a lot of weapons in town—I called back to the VPVN house and told them not to watch the celebration on the roof as they had planned. The next morning there were two spent rounds on the roof. The surgical team never got to the party that night, since the girl was the first of six casualties.

The next afternoon, which was Tet, I had dinner with Ba Nam, the head nurse on one of the medical wards, and her husband, father, and nine children. Only one of the children spoke English and I couldn't speak Vietnamese or French, but they were wonderful and made me feel a part of their family. They provided me some insight into the traditions of Tet.

Tet in 1967 had been a good time to be in Can Tho, so I

planned to return in time for Tet of '68. Various problems at our medical school prevented me from getting back a few weeks before Tet as planned, and the Tet offensive delayed things even more, so I didn't get back until about two weeks afterwards. There were still gunships over Saigon each night and plenty of evidence of the fighting in Cho Lon. Since I had been there before and things were a little mixed up, they gave me my papers and took me to the airport and told me to hitch a ride on a military plane going to Can Tho.

Flying into town, you could see the university building had been destroyed and part of the city, to within a few blocks of the hospital, had been leveled. That first night they walked about forty rockets up our street and followed it about ten minutes later with air bursts, but luckily we didn't have many casualties. Again there was an excellent air force team of surgeons, VPVN surgeons, and an ophthalmologist. It obviously wasn't the same, however, and everyone was very tense. The number of civilian casualties had increased to over seven hundred a month and one Vietnamese anesthesiologist had been called off to the military, so the surgeons were understaffed and very upset.

For my part there were fewer patients, and no one further than seven to eight klicks out of town came in for care. A Vietnamese doctor was taking care of the pediatric patients, which formed the bulk of the patients I had seen before, so this decreased the patient load even more. There were two American laboratory technicians at the hospitals, however, who were excellent, and our diagnostic ability was better.

Dr. Douglas was still in Can Tho, and because there was less to do in our hospital, he sent me around to all the civilian provincial hospitals in the Delta to see what was happening. Each hospital had two to five or more young American military doctors taking care of the civilian patients. Many were Berry Planners, and all were some of the best products of American medical education. Many of the towns had extensive signs of the recent fighting and were full of refugees. The VC were still around in the countryside, but the towns were all safely under government control. The doctors were conducting business as usual and doing a good job with what they had.

Since the surgical team was swamped and I wasn't, Dr. Hernandez, who was in charge of the air force surgical team, asked if I would also take care of the burn ward. By our standards it was unreal. Patients were kept on cots covered with cane mats which had newspapers on top that could be changed as needed. The patients' families were instructed on how to help with the bedding. Techniques were not very sterile, but they seemed to do well. The patients did not make a sound when we removed the dead tissue. It had to be very painful. They were a truly amazing people.

One day I came back early before the afternoon siesta was over and there were three children in the emergency room who had been burned. An American news photographer came in and started taking pictures. Right after Tet there were a lot of American and foreign reporters and photographers in town. I was paying attention to the children and the interpreter to find out what had happened, and it took me a while to realize the photographer was talking to me about the children having been burned by napalm. When I told him that the three had been burned in their home from an accidental stove fire, he lost all interest in the children. He didn't seem to be concerned that they were badly burned and that one of them would later die. A lot of the reporters who were there then were that way.

Many wanted to give the American and the South Vietnamese military a bad image, but none of them seemed to have a real concern about the patients or wanted to know about the people.

Bird Dog

Terry Dyke
Aydelotte . . . Pleiku, 1967–68
Reconnaissance Pilot, 219th Aviation Company

At K-State I had to take ROTC. It was required. I had the worst attendance record in the history of ROTC. It was a joke. The military was the farthest thing from my mind. About my junior year, my future brother-in-law, who was in the military, told me, "You're making a big mistake not going to advance ROTC. That way you'll be an officer and in control when you go to Vietnam. And you're going to Vietnam." This was 1963, and not that much was going on in Vietnam. I wasn't sure I believed him, but I respected his foresight in other matters. I signed up for advance ROTC.

They laughed me down. I shaped up. I didn't become gung ho, but I shined my shoes. Somehow I got in. Maybe nobody else wanted it. That last year interested me. I wanted them to teach me to fly, but for that I had to stay an extra year. But heck, I thought, with that added year maybe Vietnam would go away.

We all knew Vietnam orders were coming in flight

school. But you know, you don't really expect something till it's actually here. When they came, I got that cold, clammy all-alone-ness, like laughing in court and then realizing, "They're gonna hang you, buddy." It was heavy news. I must have turned chalky white. I was just married, too.

Flying Bird Dog, it gave you a good feeling to help out troops in trouble on the ground. The O-1 Bird Dog was a vintage Cessna tail dragger, two tandem seats, high wing, slow but highly maneuverable, with plenty of power. An old throwback to World War II and Korea, when it was the L-19, the old dog was still a good trick for aerial observation since the U.S. owned the sky over Nam. We flew in support of the Fourth Infantry mostly. The grunts would give us a call and we'd get a briefing at DTOC. They'd give me an FO. I'd just have to hope he knew his stuff and wouldn't throw up when the flying got sticky. Sometimes you got a good one.

It could get sticky. I would fly in and out of the trees. There was a kill zone at between 200 feet and about 1,500 feet where you'd better not fly. Above that or below it, you were pretty safe. The air force used gray bird dogs as forward air controllers. They had definite orders not to fly below 1,500 feet, which they followed. But they lost a bunch of them up there. I felt safe on the treetops; the air force would get it right through the butt. We were supposed to wear armored vests, but taking a cue from the USAF, we would sit on them instead. They were uncomfortable and added weight to the plane. Our mission was mainly to provide artillery support and gunships, but from talking to the air force guys in the O clubs, I was able to pick up on their frequencies. When I had those, I could call in jets as well. I believed in using whatever I could when the grunts were getting hit.

We could stay on station a long time. Our little planes had tremendous staying power: four hours. Sometimes I flew ten or fifteen feet above the canopy of the jungle looking for the enemy's position. We would find them and pull back and watch the artillery hit them. "You're right on 'em, baby." This wasn't that dangerous. They could hear you coming, but by the time you came out of the trees, you were over their heads and back into the trees before they could pop you.

In contact, the cockpit was a mess. I filled the windshield with numbers, frequencies, and coordinates, using a grease pencil. I had maps laying spread out on my lap. I always had a cigarette in my mouth, and I was constantly talking on the radio. Sometimes it was like the flying in a 3-D movie. Up and down, rolling around. Flying in and out of canyons looking for sampans. Wild.

Our 219th Aviation Company was called the Headhunters. It was the other way around. We were told by our hoochmaids that there was a price on our heads. But we figured the enemy had orders not to fire at a bird dog until the cat was out of the bag. We heard it was SOP for the enemy to shoot the guy who shot at a bird dog. We were like the point man: don't fire on him and give away your position.

I wasn't political. I wanted to believe we were doing the right thing and that we were winning the war, but during Tet I began to have doubts. I flew over columns of NVA soldiers marching down the roads into villages and towns. It looked like the Civil War. How can they keep coming back if we're beating them so badly? I began to think we might actually be losing big despite being told we were winning.

An Education

Willie Homer
Durant . . . Cu Chi, 1968.
Infantryman, Third of the Seventeenth Air Cavalry

I wasn't taking college seriously. I was interested in having a good time, so I flunked out and was drafted. The war didn't mean much to me at the time. I don't think I even knew where Vietnam was. The war wasn't politics to me. As I said, it didn't mean that much except I knew there was fighting going on and somebody was trying to beat us.

The army was an education. I was raised to believe in Mom, apple pie, and fighting for your country, so I wanted to serve, I wanted to go. But also it was like I had been raised in a closet. I had never been out of Durant except for football games, really, and I had a lot to learn. I had been brought up to think, and had always believed, that if you worked hard and did right you would be rewarded. I went in believing, I don't know, that people would be proud, would be honorable. But I found out that in the army that wasn't so. There, if you worked hard, you were just given more work. The second or third day in camp they asked for volunteers; they didn't say for what. Well, I believed in serving, so I volunteered. It was for KP. Hard, tiring work. I soon learned that to make it in the army you had to learn how to lie, and sneak around, and cheat, and sham—or get the shaft. Of course, from the beginning I knew I was going to Vietnam. I wanted to go by then. I wanted to be a grunt. When they told me I was going, it didn't have much impact on me. I had been expecting it. The only difficult time was at the airport when I was leaving. Everybody was crying: my wife, Mom, and me.

My first impression of the country in Vietnam was that it was kind of neat, in the same sense that it would have been neat to see how it was in the Old West. I mean the people were dressed funny and talked funny and were so different from us. The countryside was beautiful, and there were so many woods. I didn't think about what the war was doing to the people or about the poverty. I just didn't think about any of that. I believed I was a good soldier, and I believed in going to fight. I had pride in that, and that was mostly what I thought about.

From my AIT unit a lot of us had been sent over together so the first few days in-country weren't too bad. We burned shit and waited together for the orders to whatever line unit we'd be sent.

When we got to our unit we found that not all of us would have to go to the field. Some jobs had opened up in the rear area, and some of us new guys would fill them. They decided on letting the married guys be the ones for the jobs. They put our names in a hat. My name was one of the ones drawn. I was going to stay in the rear. One of the married guys, a guy I had been in training with, he started crying and went to load up his stuff to go to the field. The choppers were waiting. I remember sitting on my duffel bag doing some thinking, "Is this what I want? Do I want to stay back here?" I went up to the guy who had drawn the names. "Could I talk to you a minute?" I said to him. We went over and I told him I thought I'd just as soon go on out to the bush and could he give my place in the rear to that other man? Yeah, it was okay. Load up.

The choppers left without me, and I had to catch a ride to the forward base in a jeep. I manned the 60 all the way, and that was my first feeling that I was actually going into battle.

It seemed strangely like a game. We had guns, they had guns, we were here, the enemy was out there. What wasn't a game—and what impressed me and put me in awe—was some of the things we were able to do. Especially with artillery and gunships. I couldn't get over how accurate our artillery could be sometimes. We would call it in and then here it would come, right where we wanted it, as close as fifty meters from us, on top of the enemy. You could hear the shrapnel whistling over your head in the trees. The Cobras scared me. They were so bad I often wondered what the enemy was thinking while the gunship made his runs on them. Sometimes Cobras would come help us when we were caught out in the middle of the open area. And you know, when he started his run, he couldn't tell the difference in us and the enemy. He couldn't recognize us. He would build up for his power dive, and by the time he would break over and dive we would be scrambling to get out a marker for him to see us and not blow us away.

The very first time I went out on patrol we were hit. A booby trap went off, a grenade, and the guy right in front of me, my friend, took all of it. He was hurt bad. Five or six other guys were hit, but I didn't have a scratch on me. It had gotten everybody but me. My friend had blocked me.

We went on ambush. We'd been humping all day long, and then we were setting up a night ambush. This was foolish. We had been walking all over the area that day and the enemy had been watching us, so our ambush was easy to pinpoint.

It was November 3, 1968. It was midnight. I know because I had just come off watch. The old sergeant and a kid and me from AIT were sitting at the corner of the L-shaped ambush. I had just lain down in the bamboo cane. One of our guys was smoking, and I guess that drew the first fire. I raised up immediately. The sergeant grabbed me and said, "Let's go." He went first, I went second, the kid went last. We jumped over the dike into the rice paddy. Into the water. We lay in the water and fired in the dark.

After a while the kid said to me, "I think I've been hit." I thought, "Well, that's pretty dumb. Seems like you'd know if you'd been hit or not." He turned out to be shot. That started me thinking that if he was hit maybe I was too. I reached up to my head and shoulder, but I couldn't feel them. I felt wetness, but I didn't know if it was blood, since I was already in water.

The sergeant got a medic and he looked at us. I was hit, all right, but I didn't know how bad. I didn't know but what my head was blown off. The medic laid me down and began treating me. I just lay there, praying. I kept a small Bible in my heart pocket. I touched it. I wondered about dying.

The firefight didn't last long. The enemy had come in sampans, hit us hard, then got back out.

The choppers began to come for the wounded. The medics came in. They had been somewhere else, in another firefight somewhere else, and they loaded me and the kid on a chopper full of bodies from that fight. Dead people filled the bottom of the helicopter. They just threw us in on top of them. I was afraid to move because someone might still be alive beneath me. It was frightening. I didn't know if I was dying. The medic had not told me how bad I was hurt. He didn't tell me anything. On the ride back in the night there was no one to talk to but the dead bodies. I lay there scared and cold.

They kept me two weeks in a field hospital. They were afraid to move me because they couldn't find the bullet. I was scared every day. I felt like crying. I had the sense of dying. Finally, they had to move me. To Japan. There they found the bullet. They slit my neck and found it lodged an inch from my spine.

I was lucky. I think about that all the time. Why was I spared? Twice I was spared: once when my friend took the grenade blast and then the bullet missing my spine. Another curious thing. Sometime later I found out that every- body in my company—except those hurt by the grenade and the sergeant and the kid and me—ended up being killed before it was all over. We were the only ones to make it back.

From Japan they sent me back to the States. I thought I might be going back to Vietnam since I was hit my third month in-country and I had a lot of time left. I was scared, but I would have gone back if they had asked me. But no one asked me.

I spent three months in the hospital at Fort Sill, and because of my family and friends and the way they treated me, I wasn't aware of the attitude people were beginning to display to Vietnam veterans. My family and friends were very proud. To them, it was that I had been very far away fighting for my country. It wasn't until my leave was over and I went back to duty in the States that I began to see that people hated you for being in Vietnam. It was very discouraging. I got to where I didn't care anymore.

Today I'm glad the movies are out about Vietnam, if for no other reason than to show people how bad it was. I'm not sure if the people back home actually knew how tough it was. Because of some of the press, I think some people thought we were having a good time over there.

There are some things I will always remember about the experience, things that I used to try to blank out, things you could tell people but they would never understand. Things like the leeches and what they would do to your body if you didn't get them off in time. Things like being scared, your emotions. Hopefully, someday people will begin to realize what we went through.

PART TWO

Another Kind Of Wind

Don't Shoot, Charlie's Comin'

Stephen Redman
Kellyville . . . Pleiku, 1966
Infantryman, Twenty-fifth Infantry Division

We had come in. We weren't back at the base camp, but we were in. We were in a supposedly secure area. You know what I'm sayin' on this so-called secure area. The next day we was goin' out, and we knew we were going to find somethin' by what the captain told us. Guys were sitting around that night asking a lot of questions, and there was guys going around carryin' Bibles. We spent most of that night gettin' ready, mainly making sure our guns were clean.

We ran into what we thought we was goin' to run into. Another company, C Company, was a little ways behind us. We came back from this contact without losing too many men 'cause we were ready for them. But returning to the base camp, we steered around this mountain that took us right on to the Cambodian border.

Right there we found what we'd been lookin' for for six months: this one big unit of NVA supposed to be operating in this area. We never could catch them. This time they didn't run. The other company had left us. They were a long way from us when we hit the NVA, or I should say, when they hit us.

When it was all over, we had something like a hundred

and twenty-two, twenty-three men go in there with us, and only twelve of us walked out. The rest went out in bags or were flown out wounded. I said I ain't gonna make it. When it started, I fired two magazines, and that worthless piece of junk, my M-16, jammed on me. You know what I felt like. I said now what am I gonna do? And I looked around and our medic had got shot down, and I went to try to help him, and all he could say was, "My men are goin' down. I gotta go." I said, "You ain't goin' nowhere," and I took his bag away from him. I was runnin' around like I was the medic, pullin' guys back, patchin' them up and so forth, takin' care of 'em best I could with what I had, which was nothin'.

Somebody started yellin', "Don't shoot, Charlie's comin', don't shoot, Charlie's comin'." I said how 'bout that? Here we are, tryin' as hard as we can to kill Charlie, and now they're yellin' not to shoot. Well, we'd forgot about C Company, Charlie Company. Later on I talked to their lead man 'cause I didn't see how they got to us so fast. I mean, it took us a good forty-five minutes to get here and they got here in about fifteen, it seemed like. He told me they all ran fast as they could. Charlie Company ran over the hill and saved us.

I'll never forget that day. It was three days after Veterans' Day, the old Veterans' Day. I sat last year with tears in my eyes when I thought about it.

Why'd I go? I thought it was the right thing to do. I was eighteen years old. It was what you were supposed to do, y'know. We all wanted to go in my unit. We had been together in Hawaii. That's one good thing. Early, when I went to Nam, you didn't have to go by yourself. We went together, and I lost a lot of good buddies.

We were stationed in Hawaii, and the colonel called a

meeting with a whole bunch of us in the mess hall for coffee. He said, "Men, we just got orders for Vietnam." We all stood up and let out a yell. We were ready to go. 'Course when we got there we thought something else. I was nineteen when I got to country. I was a young man.

I think something ought to be done to those who went to Canada and those war protesters. I served. They should have had to serve or be punished. A planeload of us come back from Nam, and we kissed the ground at the airport, and there was some of these hippies yellin' at us and callin' us killers. The MPs moved in to come between us, and this E-7 who was on our flight held his hand out to the MPs. He said, "Don't bother. Let these boys handle them." Well, sir, we took out after them, and you should have seen them hippies run.

The Sniper

Bob Ford
Shawnee . . . Hue, 1967–68
Helicopter Pilot, 282d Assault Squadron

During Tet it was so terrible at Hue, and since the MACV compound where we lived was so small, even the pilots were issued M-16s and always manned a position on the perimeter during ground attacks. The rockets came in so loud they would scramble your brains. It was hard to think.

During the third day of an NVA attack, an Aussie friend came to get me on the wire. His name was Ford, too, Desi Ford. He called me Fordy. We were friends because I had once flown in to get him out of a tough situation when he was badly wounded. He always said that I saved his Australian manhood.

He said, "You wanna shoot one, then, mate?" He pointed about two hundred meters away where a sniper had been firing at us from the top of a palm tree for a long time without us knowing exactly where he was. I followed Desi, and we crept along with our heads down until we reached a concealed place where I could get a good look at the tree. I emptied an eighteen round clip into the tree and Desi said, "Good shooting, Fordy, but that's the wrong tree." He pointed to the tree just to the left. I jammed in another loaded clip. I have to say my adrenaline was sky high. The sniper had been doing a lot of damage to a lot of GIs. I shot him. Desi hugged me like I was his kid brother.

Shooting At Bushes,
Bushes Shooting Back

Max Dippel
Clinton . . . Phouc Vinh, Danang, 1971–72
Infantryman, First Cavalry Division, Americal Division

"Good morning, Vietnam! This is the Armed Forces, Vietnam, Station AFVN, serving the American fighting man from the Delta to the DMZ, with transmitters in Quang Tri, Danang, Qui Nhon, Pleiku, and Nha Trang, and with a key network station in Saigon, Vietnam."

I wish I'd taped that so I could play it today. That sound is one of my most vivid memories of Vietnam. It was part of the absurdity. It was like they had to provide us with everything we had at home when we were out of the bush. As if the PXs the size of Safeways, movie theaters, cheeseburgers, pizza shacks, and bars weren't enough, they gave us a rock-and-roll station so we could keep up on all the latest tunes.

First two months in-country, I wasn't scared. A lot of it was being hot, tired, thirsty, and bored. I was with the First Cav, and the talk was that the cav had their stuff together, they had kicked Chuck's rear, and he was hurtin'. Wouldn't mess with the cav. For me at first the jungle meant killing time, getting eyeballed as the new guy, trying not to mess up. It was a lot like camping out: just an adjustment to a new environment. Of course as a grunt I wasn't let in on the grand scheme of things. I had no idea of goals on any level. It was just hump it here, hump it there, hack it through a wall of green.

My first combat assault was also my first contact. Waiting for the helicopters to come get us, I couldn't shake the feeling that it was like riding out to work. They prepped the LZ, blew it all to hell. It was awesome, so exciting, but frightening, too.

After we were out about a week, my platoon went on a patrol. We walked single file. The rear of our march saw movement. It was the tail end of the enemy. We were passing each other, parallel to each other, just meters away in the thick jungle. Someone fired, and the firefight broke out. It sounded like six hundred machine guns firing. We just fired into the brush around us. It was, son of a gun, shoot at the bushes and the bushes shoot back! This went on for a while until someone yelled, "Wait a minute!" Our firefight was with another platoon of grunts.

The change to the Americal brought changes of another kind. Where the cav seemed to have it together, the Americal lacked confidence by the time I got there. There was a lot of shamming. The 196th was supposedly coming out of one of the worst beatings they'd had in the war.

We humped so much equipment. People who have never had to be responsible for their own water and carry it themselves have no idea just how heavy water is. In addition to food, ammo, and my weapon, I carried eleven quarts of water. That's a lot, but I am a big person. We got resupplied on a regular basis with the First Cav. You know, they were air mobile. I bet the whole Americal Division didn't have two helicopters! We couldn't count on resupplies with the Americal. Sometimes they came, sometimes they didn't. When they came, we got our SPs and one can of hot Black Label. But when they didn't come, too bad. I remember making tomato soup out of ketchup, onion, and water.

About dusk one night I felt the call so I took my entrenching tool and my weapon and left the perimeter. You always had to leave the perimeter out of regard for your buddies. One night in the cav I had to go. I thought I was far enough out, and I let fly, finished up, and crept back to my place and sacked out. Next morning I heard one guy not too far away waking up. He sniffed real hard, then he started yelling, "Damn, somebody went all over me!" This time I got far enough out. There was enough light barely to see. I was finishing my job when I heard these guys talking. Too loud, I thought. Guys ought to try to be a little quieter out in the bush. Then I realized, it wasn't English these guys were speaking. These were gooks! Oh, man. I ran back in and started telling guys there's gooks right out there. Some believed me, some didn't. You know how that kind of confusion goes. I finally got the platoon sergeant to believe, and we went out to look.

They were on a trail right above our heads. They could have looked down and seen us. They were NVA. It was so surrealistic. I swear it was just like a dang Bugs Bunny cartoon. These guys were carrying trees as camouflage like in a cartoon—you know, the kind where the bad guy holds a tree in front of him as if the whole world couldn't see what was really happening. They had branches in their armpits. It was funny despite the fact there were beaucoup of them and they had the higher ground.

We went into a place that was a notorious NVA stronghold on the Que Son ridge outside Danang. It was beautiful. Rice paddies were staircased right up the side of the mountain. Because of the rice paddies there was no place for cover except behind the dikes. There was no place to bed down in case you stopped there for the night. We had an incompetent for a lieutenant, and of course this is just where he decided we'd spend the night. There we were, right beneath the ridge, out in the open, in clear view of God and everybody. We were tired and a little bit lazy, but we all knew better.

My buddy and I rigged up our sleeping area. It was raining so we covered our mosquito nets with a poncho liner. I don't know what time of night it was when the NVA hit us, but they hit us with a lot of stuff. RPGs, automatic fire. My buddy rolled out of our makeshift tent and rolled over the dike into the rice paddy, just hanging onto the ridge. He caused the tent to collapse and I got tangled up in it. I was caught. I rustled around, thinking, "Well, I gotta get outta here." Rounds were hitting all over and I'm caught like a fish in a net. Everyone else is behind the dikes, below the ridge. I realized the gooks could probably see me thrashing around, and pretty soon they would kill me. I got this thought in my head: Don't move. Just lay still and they won't be able to see you. I could hear them. I was afraid to lift the poncho 'cause I knew if I did I'd be looking right into a gook's face. I had a feeling of being all alone out there. I had a fear of dying alone.

We secured the area finally and counted noses. They thought I was gone. It was a lull. It was going to be our worst day. The medevacs came in for the wounded. We were in such an exposed position, it was gonna hit the fan. It did. Two RPGs hit one chopper; guys were hurt bad. Again there was a lot of shooting at bushes, the bushes shooting back. I helped carry Robertson to a chopper, and he kept asking me, "Max, did they get me? Max, did they get me?"

Crossing the River

Gary LaBass
Bixby . . . Chu Lai, 1970–71
Infantryman, Americal Division

They sent us out through Khe Sanh Valley on a sweep with tracks—you know, Sheridans and APCs—and we thought this was going to be a holiday. I mean we were used to humping and sweating meter by meter in the jungle, and here we were, getting a ride, not having to tote those heavy rucks. Going through this wide, open, beautiful valley where we could see all around us for miles and miles. No way gooks were gonna slip up on us.

First day was great. We rode along with a nice breeze. Everybody felt good; this was a change. Only incident all day was one of the APCs lost a track, and it happened to be the one I was on. Three other vehicles stayed behind with us and we had to make a night logger there and get the track fixed. We caught up the next day where the valley narrowed and we crossed a river. Of course the easy time was too good to be true. As soon as we got on the other side of the river, we started taking fire and mortars. A lot of it.

The going was very slow that day and the third day. We took heavy fire and mortars. The way it was with me and all the other grunts I ever talked to, if you weren't a platoon leader or an RTO so you could monitor the radio, you didn't ever know what was going on, what you were expected to do, what was going to be waiting for you when you got there. Why? When? Where? You knew How? because How? was up one hill and down it, slog step at a time, sweat and puff. It was the same on this operation. No one asked us. No one told us. It was crazy.

I looked up once and the CO had a platoon off the tracks and on line against a bunker line. On line! Real AIT stuff. A jerk move. One dink just waited until the line passed, and he popped up and got off a lot of shots. Ping. Ping. Ping. He hit a bunch of guys with their backs turned. He hit the CO, and he didn't come back. That was good. He was a screw-up of a commander. We found out later the CO put himself up for the Distinguished Service Cross.

We wandered around, and finally we were going to get back on the other side of the river. And man, we were all glad of that. That was the safe ground. Just shows you how screwed up it got sometimes. In our minds, it was like: before we crossed the river, we had it made, we crossed the river and all hell broke loose, so it figures, we get back across we're safe again.

We were lax. I'll tell you how easy we're taking it. The tracks are parked on line, and we're on top reading *Stars and Stripes*— y'know, catching up on what's happening. I mean we're at ease.

Out of nowhere there's this huge explosion. The Sheridan three tracks in front is destroyed, just a blazing and smoking hull. I look to my left, and behind a tree I see one puff of smoke and there's an RPG heading for the track I'm sitting on. I knew I was a dead man. I couldn't move. It hits below my feet and thirteen guys are splattered by shrapnel. It all missed me except for my foot. It all blew out and up and got everybody around me. My boot is smoking, and there are two holes through it.

We get the AO secured and there's a dust-off coming. I'm feeling better about everything. I'm getting out of the field. I wanted out for a few days. Who wouldn't? The new CO comes over to me. "Can you walk?" he says. "We need you."

My foot was starting to bother me, and of course I knew what he was getting at. There were about four guys who had to be dusted off. That's the thing about it. No one was ever going to say anything to you about trying to get out of the field. Everybody wanted out. There it was. I told him, "I'll be okay."

What're you gonna do? I'm no hero. Not gung ho. But I had buddies out there, and it would just make it that much tougher on them.

Lifers didn't go to the field much. We got back to the firebase and we were mad. We sat around and talked, glad to be out for a day, but mad. We were saying things like, "No way we're going back in there." "We just ain't going, that's all!" And we had this sergeant major. All he could tell us, strutting around, was, "I been in three wars, and there ain't nothing so bad a five-hundred-pound bomb can't take care of."

"Get a load of this guy," I thought. "Let's see him get out there in the field. Talk is cheap." Well, he was going out with us the next day, when we were going back in to do it right. And, the crazy thing is, he saved my life.

The CO asked me if I thought I could go. My foot had swollen, and I wasn't getting around too great. We were going back in there where we had caught all the hell, this time without the tracks. We would walk! By the book. One platoon on line one side of the road, another platoon the other side, headquarters down the middle of the road.

"You'll be with me," the captain said. "It'll be the easiest walking. Can you make it? I'll put you right behind me and the RTO. What'ya say?"

Then the sergeant major spoke up, and he told the captain, "He can walk, but if we get hit, he's not going to be able to move very good. He better stay here."

So the lifer kept me from going out. The company got hit very soon down the road, and of course it was headquarters that was hit the hardest. The CO was killed. He was hit in the neck. He was a good man. The radioman was hit, and the third guy, the guy that would've been me, was killed.

Sergeant major, the tough guy. My buddies said he lost it. He was so scared his butt was tightened up so you couldn't have driven a nail in there with a sledgehammer.

War Machine
And the Smell Of Fear

David Samples
Sapulpa . . . Dong Ha, 1966–67
Seabee, U.S. Navy Mobile Construction

The war was like a machine, a machine to do one thing and do it very effectively: destroy people. It was out of control and chewed up people. The thing is, it didn't just chew up flesh; it chewed up human will. You could hear it when someone's will snapped. It was like a spring wound too tight. It was a sound you never forget. Like a whimper, but loud, too. And that look of desperation and defeat. Fear gripped at our souls.

Seconds were like eternity. The monsoon rains were thick, but so were the rockets, the mortars, the artillery. On the DMZ, we dreamed of escaping—escaping the fear.

Those broken wills screamed of fear. We learned to live minute by minute. Who thought of tomorrow? Fear was the thing we feared the most. Fear is terrible. It disables you. It can break you.

You know, you could get away from it for a while and you almost felt safe. You could almost begin to look forward to tomorrow again. And then that machine was back on top of us, and there was that smell again. The smell of fear. To me it was rancid, stank worse than rotten flesh. Again you had to reduce yourself to minute by minute. That machine rolled.

Riverboat

Bill Poffenberger
Tulsa . . . Mekong Delta, 1970–71
Patrol Boat Repair Barge, U.S. Navy

We might as well have been in the jungle. We were on the river between Tam Chau and the Cambodian border. Ours was a barge that repaired the Cambodian and the Vietnamese boats. We also supported the helicopter units of that area. We worked on boats and helicopters, made supply runs, and supported the Filipino convoys that went up the river to Phnom Penh.

My closest friends were the Cambodians. They were beautiful people. The Cambodians and the Vietnamese stayed on separate sides of the boat. They wouldn't mingle. I stayed on the Cambodian side. They would do anything for you. I gave them cigarettes, and they gave me an AK-47 and an SKS. The thing about the Cambodians, they were wanting to win the damned war.

Snipers hit us a lot, and it was a helpless feeling because we couldn't move unless a tug helped us. I would get scared. I'd have butterflies, and I would shake. Sometimes I would end up somewhere on the boat and I couldn't remember how I got there. I fired back, but I didn't know what the hell I was shooting at. There were times I would go with the Cambodians on a patrol boat and they would go after the snipers. The goddamn Vietnamese who were supposed to be with us would run the other way. It really pissed me off. It gave me a bad attitude about them.

We were hit one night when a rocket took out a helicopter and went through the dining area. I didn't think I would come home that night. All hell broke out on both banks of the river. Tracers filled the air, and they called in the helicopters and the Black Pony (the Navy Light Attack Squadron) and even the Dragon—Puff the Magic Dragon we called him. The whole Cambodian side looked like a gigantic fireworks display.

I was scared. We had .50-cals on the deck. On the stern we had what was called a Honeywell, an M-79 rapid-fire grenade launcher, rigged up. Being scared, I shot back like hell, not knowing anything that I might be hitting.

The Village

Wilbert Brown
Tulsa . . . Pleiku, 1966
Infantry Scout, Twenty-fifth Infantry Division

Our unit was extremely special, but we weren't highly decorated because bravery was the natural order of our company. We were 75 percent minority: blacks, Puerto Ricans, Chicanos, Indians. We didn't have many whites, but the CO, the first sergeant, and the RTO were white.

Often we were called upon to perform unusual missions. Intelligence sent us a difficult one. The VC were going to hit a village that had been friendly to us. As a crack unit, we were to go in, circle the village, and protect the people.

Each unit was assigned a sector outside the village wall to secure and hold against attack. Just before dark we dug our foxholes and set in for the attack. We were ready. Then, for some unknown reason, the word came in over the radio for all the units to shift sectors. So we packed up in a hurry and moved quickly in the dark to a sector originally set up by some white guys. We couldn't believe what we saw when we got there. They hadn't dug in at all! No foxholes, no fighting positions, nothing, no protection. It blew our minds. There we were, the jungle to our front, the ten-foot-high wall to our backs, and no cover. We were out in the open, easy targets.

At midnight, that's when it hit. The VC began to walk mortars all the way around the village, in on top of the American positions. You could just hear them coming, walking right toward you. You were helpless. And then, if things weren't already in bad enough shape, some nut on the other side of the village started popping flares. Our position was totally exposed.

In the light of the flares I looked around me. There were two guys to my right who were not hit, and there were two guys to the left still moving. Everybody else in our sector was wounded or dead. We heard the noises of the VC in the bush, getting ready to move on us. We got up and looked at each other. "Is this it?" we seemed to be thinking among ourselves. We raised our rifles for the ground attack. The noises in the jungle were getting louder. We braced ourselves.

A blaring noise came out over the jungle tops. It was a loud-speaker, y'know, like a public-address system. An eerie scene. Then a VC spoke into the loudspeaker in good

English. "Hey, GI," he said, "not tonight." And they left. They were taunting us, laughing at us, playing our game.

The units began rounding up, but the five of us were still standing there by our wounded, ready to fight, when they found us.

Another Kind of Wind

Stan Beesley
Tecumseh . . . Phouc Vinh, 1970–71
Reconnaissance Scout, Seventy-fifth Infantry Rangers

It was a hot spring night and I was in college—carefree and not worried about the war—when I had a dream about Vietnam. I dreamed about going there. To be honest, I had not really thought much about the war. Not that I wasn't concerned. I mean, it was just that I was in college, and I had never really thought of myself as ever having to go. I considered myself fairly mature and thoughtful. But actually I was a kid and full of it.

In the dorm we had stayed up late with the windows open and the radios on because there were tornado alerts out. The dream was so vivid. I was outside myself watching as I moved down a trail in the jungle. I was dressed in camouflage fatigues (in my dream I didn't know what they were; I never saw cammies until I got into the Ranger company and was issued a pair) and I was creeping along very stealthily. I was carrying my weapon the proper way and everything. You gotta understand, at the time I knew next to nothing about Vietnam and the army and weapons, but there I was, doing everything like it was supposed to be done. It was so real. Even the smell. The wind was hushed as it moved through the branches and leaves of the jungle canopy. I followed the back of the soldier in front of me. I had the strong sense that a soldier followed me, but I didn't see one in my dream. The whole scene was very quiet and purposeful.

In the morning I woke and sat on the edge of my bed. I felt very calm about it, as if some important issue had been settled. My roommate was getting dressed. I said to him, "I'm going to Vietnam." Just like that. He looked at me real funny, as if to say, "Yeah, right," and went on dressing.

I didn't really dwell on the dream. It sounded so crazy and out of place in that peaceful campus setting: pretty girls passing beneath your window, spring football practice, afternoons at the river. But I kept it with me, and in quiet times I would remember it.

Two years and what seemed like a lifetime later, my team was on a mission near the Cambodian border. We were going down this well-used trail. The jungle was thick. The monsoon was coming up, and the clouds covered half the sky. We shouldn't have been on the trail—usually we wouldn't get on a trail—but we had to hurry to get to the LZ and be extracted before the rains hit. We moved quickly but quietly, straining our eyes into the brush for an ambush. Then it hit me hard. This was my dream. Here it was, happening exactly like I'd seen it so much earlier. I started laughing. I couldn't help it. I mean I never held much with the spiritual, but here I was. I laughed and shook my head all the way to the LZ. We sat around the LZ waiting for the chopper, and the TL came over and asked what was wrong with me back on the trail, and I told him about the dream. He just shook his head like I was nuts and said, "Yeah, right."

At the Ninetieth Replacement Center at Long Binh, while I waited and wondered with hundreds of others just in-country, I spent three days on bunker guard. All kinds of emotions ran through me. My nerves were jangled from loss of sleep between Oakland, Hawaii, Okinawa, and Bien Hoa. I expected my position to be overrun with VC. It was supposed to be a secure area, but, hey, who is kidding whom? Everyone knows there is no such thing as secure in Vietnam. That first day while lined up in front of a hootch receiving bedding, I had seen three rounds of incoming land between the mess hall and basketball court. We new guys stood there and stared at the large puffs of smoke and dust and never moved until a red-faced officer ran out of the mess and screamed at us.

I looked out the slit of the bunker and thought every hootch maid, barber, and bar girl who walked by was going to suddenly pull out a grenade and toss it at me. I had the sensation that this is war. Later, when looking back, I realized it was probably crazy putting all of us cherries in those bunkers with claymores, M-60s, M-79s, and M-16s in such a populated area. Given our emotional state, it was a wonder a lot of people weren't killed.

Those three days my eyes hurt from straining them to stare at the people who streamed by on the highway. It was so mysterious and foreign, so different. There was the smell of diesel and burning shit, the sounds of the scooters and lambrettas with their sewing-machine engines. It was crazy how the Vietnamese crowded onto the vehicles. A bus designed to hold forty usually carried more than a hundred, and they were crammed in the windows and on top among the racks with their pigs and chickens. A three-wheel lambretta that was supposed to carry two passengers might have eight or nine people jammed into the back. All day long there was a river of people up and down that road, coming and going from the French-built factory and the U.S. base. I kept a hand on the butt of the 60 and stared out at the beautiful girls in their ao-dais and at the mamasans in their black pajamas, and I wondered if I was going to stay alive for a whole year.

The sergeant of the guard the last day was a lifer cook, and he seemed to me to know a lot about the whole thing—Vietnam and the people—as he drove me out to my bunker. I wanted to hear all he could tell me. It had occurred to me that the women were either young and very beautiful in their ao-dais or they were ugly, wrinkled, stooped, and very old in their silky pajamas; no women in between.

I asked the lifer about this. "You just about hit it on the head," he said. "They're either princesses or hags." I guess I looked puzzled because he went on. He turned out to be a real philosopher. "The women are all pretty here once, when they are about nineteen. Then they turn old and ugly."

I wondered how this cook had accumulated so much knowledge of the peasants, but I was so new, and everything about being here was so unreal, I figured anything was possible. I said, "But what about the chewing tobacco? All the mamasans have black teeth from the stuff."

"Ain't no chaw, cherry," the lifer said, fiddling with the .45 on his belt. "Betel nut. They start eatin' it when they lose their firstborn, which is damned early in this place, and then they are old for the rest of their lives."

My first mission I hardly even thought about the enemy.

I was more worried about screwing up. Alpha Team had been together a long time and worked well together. I was the new guy. They would be watching me, waiting for me to pull a boner.

Miller was the team leader, and he told me to stay close to him. He crept through the brush and the wait-a-minute vines and I followed close, trying to imitate him. Every time he stopped and got down, I did too. My pack was so heavy it bent me over double. Before we had gone a half-mile into the jungle, I was soaking wet from sweat. I didn't think I could make it another step. My shoulders ached from the straps, my lungs burned, and my back hurt like hell. And I thought I was in fairly good shape! I thought to myself, "I can never keep this up for the rest of the day, let alone for a whole year. I won't make it." I wanted to just quit. Sit down right there and let Charlie have me. The thing that kept me going and uncomplaining, though, was that Miller and Garcia were half my size and carrying even more weight than I was, and they were humping right along. Y'know, it was a case of "If they can do it, I can do it" and "What's the use of bitchin'?"

Somehow I made it to the end of the day, humping along, breathing hard and grunting, straining my eyes at my AO, trying to be as quiet as the rest of the team, listening to the whispers of the other men when we crowded together in a bamboo thicket or under some brush for a break. I watched every move anybody made, trying to learn the little things that I was sure would keep you alive in the jungle. I was amazed at how quiet men could be and still communicate perfectly. Without speaking, they knew when it was time to put out claymores, time to eat, time to drink water, time to get up and move.

When Miller finally decided that we would stop for the

night, I was too exhausted to care about anything. I didn't care about eating. I didn't even take off my pack. I just lay back on it. I didn't think about the enemy. I didn't want to move.

But that wasn't the way it was going to be. I was so new I hadn't even realized Miller had found a trail and that we were on NDP here because we were going to ambush the trail. We were on a little knoll overlooking the trail. As tired as I was, I perked up a little at this. The enemy was actually nearby—or had been. Miller told me to take my weapon, claymore, and web gear and follow him and Garcia. We were going to set up the ambush. All right. I felt important. I knew Garcia was a good man, and Miller was taking me along because he trusted me. Of course, later, I realized he just wanted to show me how it was done and to see how I would handle myself. But at the time I felt good and was determined that I wasn't going to screw up.

It was just like training. We low-crawled down the knoll through the bushes until we came to the trail. Sure enough, there was a trail. Miller took time to show me the footprints, and he whispered to me how many he thought had been on the trail and how recently. Much later in my tour, when I was a rear scout, I learned to read trails, and this skill saved my life many times.

It was eerie out in the open. Suddenly, I felt exposed and alone. Miller sent Garcia down the trail and he motioned for me to go up the trail. "About twenty meters— where it makes a bend there," he said. I can imagine how my eyes must have looked because he shoved me a little and grinned. "All you Okies know how to shoot, don't you? You see something, just shoot it." Yeah. Simple.

I moved up the trail and lay down at the base of a big

tree and peeked around the corner. The trail disappeared into even heavier brush. Anyone coming down the trail would be on us immediately. I thought maybe I'd better get in the kneeling position to be better prepared. I eased the safety off my weapon. Then I thought, no, I better put it on automatic. Then I thought I made too big a target, so I lay back down. My fingers cramped and I was afraid I might jerk the trigger, so I switched the safety off again. It only took Miller about ten minutes to set up the claymores, but it seemed to me like hours. I was up and down, safety off and on. I cussed Miller for putting me out here. It was too much responsibility for a cherry. What if I let a whole battalion walk up on us? What if they sneak up from behind and kill everybody else and leave me out here alone? I wondered what I was going to do if a VC actually walked down the trail. Of course I would shoot him. It was a heavy responsibility. I found out later that, above me on the knoll, Mac had the 60 pointed up the trail covering me.

When Miller got the ambush set up, we crawled back up the knoll and settled in. Wallen showed me how to cut a sleeping position out of the bushes. I was feeling better. Miller had said I did well out on the ambush. I had a little water and was thinking about eating something. This might not be so bad after all. I was with good men, we were going to ambush Charlie, I had helped, and they trusted me. I was going to make it.

It was almost dark. We slept close enough together that we could wake each other in the night by touching. Through small openings in the brush, we could observe the trail in three places. Mac was a big guy who carried the 60, and he didn't say much. That's why I sat up when he said, "Damn!" I saw him reach over one guy and grab Miller.

Then he jabbed his finger toward the trail, looking pissed. We all looked. At first I didn't see anything. Everybody else did, though, and they didn't like it. My throat went instantly dry. Garcia looked at me. He pointed and then I saw it. By the big tree where I had been on the trail there was a grenade. Somehow I had let a frag fall off my web belt, and now it lay in the middle of the trail. "Shinin' like a diamond in a goat's ass" was the way Mac put it.

Well, I had screwed up. And good. I figured these crusty vets would just blow me away and tell God I died. It didn't take long before I was one of them, and I realized they were only eighteen, nineteen, and twenty years old and just as scared every time in the jungle the same as me, but at that moment with that grenade lying out there on the trail, I assumed they wished they were minus one cherry.

Miller didn't say a word. He grabbed his weapon and low-crawled down the knoll and fetched the grenade. No harm done. He got back and flipped it to me. I realized then that Miller was not your ordinary army sergeant because before I could say I was sorry he told me, "Don't worry about it. Who doesn't make a mistake once in a while in this damn place?"

On the Bong Son Plain

Morris James
Shawnee . . . An Khe, 1967–68
Infantryman, First Cavalry Division

Craziest thing, but we took fire on our training mission. Those first two weeks in-country. We had gone through the orientation and the basic in-country training, and you know that was always topped off with a little practice patrol in the bush. Good practice, but the patrol was just outside the perimeter and you weren't supposed to get shot at, but we were.

We were close in to An Khe, this big base, and we felt safe. When the firing started, you talk about a bunch of cherry boys who didn't know what was going on! Of course we had been around a lot of firing on the ranges in training, but this was different. At first it didn't dawn on us what was happening. It all seemed so unreal.

First real mission, when it wasn't practice, was to sweep a village located on the Bong Son Plain. When we entered the village we saw total destruction. Everything was rubble. I mean there were no buildings left standing. It had been hit by air strikes, artillery, napalm. It had been hit two or three days before, and the bodies were starting to rot and bloat. The smell!

My first conscious act in that village was to pull a body out of the rubble. I pulled on an arm and it came away from the rest of the body. After a while the stench got so bad we had to put on our gas masks. But, I'll tell you, it didn't do any good. When I think of Nam, I think of that smell. Even when I first came in to Cam Ranh Bay the smell had been in the air. At the time I couldn't identify it, but after that village I knew what it was. Of course I got sick that day in the village.

First three months in-country I walked point. I wanted to. Point man carried a 12-gauge shotgun. It's funny how a man can get used to anything, how he acclimates. I felt good out in front, comfortable. When they took me off point, I didn't want to go. I felt secure when I was in the lead. Back in the line I was uneasy at first, but the old man wanted me to be his RTO. I got to where I liked that, too, because I knew everything that was going on. I could hear it on the radio.

Different units would move different distances, depending on the nature of the operation and depending on the leader. The worst humping I ever heard of was going thirty klicks in one day in the Central Highlands, and that was us.

We were on a search-and-destroy operation. We were involved in a village cordon. We moved into the village at night—early morning, actually. It was one of those kinds of missions where if anything moved it was dead meat. Well, we had a large body count, real successful. Bodies everywhere. It was such a big deal the colonel flew in with hot coffee and doughnuts. It was unreal. Guys sitting around on dead gooks drinking coffee and eating doughnuts.

The word came to mount up. First Platoon, my platoon, would move out. We would lead. We had this nineteen-year-old lieutenant, a pimply-faced guy. He got us lost. We stumbled onto this creekbed. He was so lost. He said, "Let's follow this creek and we'll eventually come out down in the valley.'' Well, of course he was right, but you never saw such a damned up-and-down, twisting, hard hump in your life. It liked to have killed me. I was carrying a full pack, rifle and ammo, plus the radio. After a while I was hurting so bad I just lost track.

We were so lost we couldn't even call the helicopters to come get us. We just humped and humped. It was rough going. Finally we got where we were supposed to be going. The captain—his name was Mallory—he had a photographic mind when it came to maps. He was amazing. He could look at a map one time, and that was it. He could tell you exactly where you were, at what coordinates, and what landmark you were getting ready to come up on. Anyway, the captain took a map and showed us where we had come from. It was over thirty klicks altogether.

Pretty soon they called us and told us to get ready to go cordon another village, and the captain put his foot down. He said, ''Not this unit, they're done in.''

Naturally, we never questioned any order. We thought we were doing the right thing. They tell us to go, we go. I never doubted that we were winning 'cause every battle I was in we always won. We were good soldiers, or at least we thought we were, and that's 90 percent of the issue. We did the job. We used to joke that our unit could walk down the Bong Son Plain with nothing but .45s and kick ass. Most of the guys really believed we could.

The only time I had a flicker of doubt about the whole war was the time we were on an LZ outside of Phu Bai and a general flew in, a two- or three-star guy. He was decked out, lookin' good. Had his own chopper. You remember how they had big trash barrels full of ice and beer and Cokes? Well, the general reached in and grabbed a beer and started jawing with us, y'know. It was cool. He wanted to be with the boys. It was a good talk. He shot us straight, I believe, about what we were doing, and then he said, "Men, if they'd quit messing around and let Westy go, turn him loose, we could march right into Hanoi." That bothered me a little. Was somebody holding us back? I thought we were giving it our all. I began to realize that it wasn't just fighting—unit against unit, country against country—there was politics involved. It changed my thinking just a little bit.

I never learned to trust gooks while I was in Nam. Outside of An Khe there was a place called Sin City. You crossed under a gate and came into an entire circular area of buildings where there were all the vices you could think of, all for the enjoyment and corruption of the GI. When we were overrun, we policed up the bodies on the wire afterward and we found the bartenders, the barbers, and the shoe-shine boys from Sin City.

Overrun. Scary. I came to the conclusion then that I was mortal after all. I wasn't invincible.

It was a scary feeling for them to break through at a place as big as An Khe. On the bunker line there was concertina wire, foo gas, and claymores. Still they got through. In waves.

When it first started, one tower near us, on the same frequency as us and TOC—the tactical operations center—called in and said they had movement in the wire. The guy called for permission to fire. TOC piddled around and wanted confirmation, told them to wait, not to shoot at anything. The guy in the tower is yelling, "There's gooks in the wire!" Still no word to fire.

Then it happened. Just like that. Flares went off and here they came. Still the tower didn't have permission to fire. That tower was the first to go in the attack. Three guys dead because TOC didn't have confirmation on movement.

It's an unbelievable sight, seeing bodies coming through the wire. Waves of them. Waves coming uphill. I grabbed my helmet and vest and me and a couple of other guys jumped up on top of a bunker. From there we had a good sight of the whole thing. Every time a flare went off, we would see the gooks running for the wire.

We blew the gas and claymores on them, and the artillery lowered the 105s to point blank and shot fléchette rounds at them. Surprisingly for all the numbers involved, it was over soon after it began. We cleaned up gooks for days. A week later we found two hiding in a chapel.

I was an old man in my unit. I turned twenty-one in a rice paddy during an eleven-hour firefight. We had come out of LZ English, and Intelligence told us we would encounter the Twenty-second NVA Regiment, and we did. They hit us hard.

We took fire from the very first. We came in on an air assault. The chopper I was on took a hit. I went out belly first in the mud. I was firing like crazy, but I didn't know where or at what. I was lying there and the crew chief grabbed my foot and pulled on it. He yelled, ''Come on. We're going.'' Somehow that bird got airborne and the pilot moved us to another LZ. He flew the crippled chopper treetop level.

This NVA unit had been in this area so long they were entrenched. They had a maze of trenches and tunnels all over the AO. They could walk around and get behind you and you would never see them until it was too late.

We had a brand-new lieutenant for this operation. He didn't even last the day. His war didn't even last one day before they shipped him home in a bag.

The thing I remember most about that day besides it

being November 1, my birthday, was me losing my helmet. You know how guys would bitch about how heavy those things were. And awkward. Couldn't wait to take them off in training. Well, that day I lost mine in the water and the mud. I felt naked without it. I lay in that mud behind a fallen palm tree the whole day and just knew I was gonna get it.

Another time in those rice paddies we were on a night patrol, an ambush. We were all set up behind one of those high dikes. Claymores out front on the trail. Ready for the gooks to didi by and we'd blow them away. We were set, man. Everything was just right. And damned if the NVA didn't come in behind us! You talk about puckered up. Gooks never came through the fields, but here they came. A big force, well armed and toting 82-mm mortars. We were exposed, our backs right to them. All we could do was lay still and hope somehow they went by without seeing us or stepping on us.

They did go by without finding us, and fortunately we didn't open up on them or it would have gone bad for us.

We got back to base feeling damned shaky, and this lieutenant we had, he was real apologetic to the CO. He kept going around saying he was sorry we didn't engage the enemy. Engage the enemy! Hell, if we had made a peep they would have wiped us out.

Heavy was our best man. I didn't know his real name, first or last. I don't think anybody did. He was just Heavy. All we knew was he was B-A-D.

Heavy was a big black dude. Y'know those stories about guys carrying a 60 around on a strap like it was a toy? Well, to Heavy that's what it must have felt like. He strapped that gun across his arm and walked with it like it was a .16. He could fire it on the run, and it didn't slow him down in the least.

Heavy liked to take it upon himself to pull one-man perimeter guard. He'd pick up the gun and lurk around and check the wire, and God help the man he found sleeping on guard. He'd say, "Now you're messin' with MY life, mother."

We were pinned down outside a village by snipers. It was so frustrating. We couldn't move. We had to keep our heads down. We didn't move for an hour and a half. I don't know what happened. I guess Heavy just got tired of it because then we heard that gun of his start barking. We all peeked up, and you know how it is: one guy goes, you gotta follow. It's the natural thing.

Heavy had this little ol' ammo bearer; Heavy made two of him. It was funny, he was so little and Heavy was so big. The guy didn't want to go toward that village, but there was Heavy taking off across the road and field with the 60, right into the gunfire. The ammo bearer was more afraid of Heavy than he was of the gooks 'cause he snuck in behind him, making sure Heavy's broad shoulders stayed in front.

Heavy kept firing rounds and the little ammo bearer kept feeding him more, and he ran right at the hootches. He didn't stop until he reached the village, and then he dropped to the ground. He had been hit three times, but it hadn't stopped him until we had all got across.

Snipers were the most frustrating thing. It made you so mad 'cause they could hurt you plus keep you down for hours. A buddy of mine, Jim Kamper, and I got some back from at least one sniper. From out of some rocks a sniper had hit our unit. He had us all pinned down. He was good, too, pinging away at us. One round kicked up the dirt by my heel where I was lying down.

After a while, nothing much was happening except this gook shooting at us, so Jim and I talked the old man into letting us go after the sniper. He threw a fit 'cause I was the RTO and he didn't want to lose me, but finally we talked him into it. He let us go, but he said, "Be careful."

Jim and I snuck our way around him and got higher on the rocks than him. We peeked over, and there was this little gook firing away with an old German rifle that was as tall as he was. Just before we fired, it couldn't do but for Kamper to holler at the gook so he would turn around and look at us.

I still have that rifle. It's an 8-mm. I disassembled it and packed it in my stuff I was taking home with me. When I got to hold baggage at the air base the guy started looking through my stuff and I thought, "Oh, no." Sometimes they checked good, sometimes not. There was a lot of things being smuggled out of country, but there were so many guys they couldn't check every single guy. I was taking a chance.

This guy was gonna check me out good. Then he saw this picture of Jean Ann. It was a big framed picture that I'd kept with me. I had packed the rifle parts underneath the picture. The guy goes, "Hey, I think I know that girl. Where's she from?" I told him, "Oklahoma," and he said that was where he was from. We got to talking and BS'ing and after a while I said, "Yeah, man, I gotta be goin'," and he just let me through.

Hell At 500 Knots

Robert Kirk
Oklahoma City . . . Danang, 1969–70
F-4 Fighter Pilot, 480th Tactical Fighter Squadron

The red of the instrument panel was the only thing showing against the total blackness of the night. My first mission in Vietnam. I'll never forget what the other pilot said to me. "Robert," he said "tonight is the night we make a killer out of you."

It was like someone took a knife and stuck it in my stomach. It couldn't have hurt any more. I didn't want to kill anyone. I hadn't wanted any part of a jet fighter. I had listed a C-135 as my preference all through training, but when I came in after my last training flight in Enid, our orders were listed on the board and mine said, "Kirk: F-4."

We were hitting a pass leading out of North Vietnam. The road through the pass led into Laos and then into South Vietnam. We tried to interdict passes up there. You can't believe the things we dropped on them: 500-, 1,000-, and 2,000-pound slick bombs and CBUs—cluster-bomb units. We carried them in canisters under our wings. We also dropped bombs with magnetic warheads. They would hit the ground but not blow up. Then a truck would run over them and boom!

This day we were dropping 500-pound slick bombs with

the magnetic warheads. We made a pass at 500 knots and 500 feet; they had to be delivered at 500 knots and 500 feet altitude. The first ship in is okay because they don't know you're coming. We were in the lead for this mission. We came smoking down this valley. I wish I could describe it. On either side of the valley there were ridges of limestone. Water had washed out caves and caverns and stalagmites on the walls. We were only 500 feet altitude, so the ridges were above our aircraft. I looked down and I thought this must be the most bombed area on the face of the earth. There were bomb craters inside bomb craters. It looked like the surface of the moon. Trees were splintered and broken, and smoky fires burned and glowed. Dante's hell. I thought, "This must be what hell looks like."

The NVA had guns in the caves, and when the aircraft made the bombing runs the guns shot back and forth at you across the valley. As lead, we went in and rousted them. Two was close behind us. They hit him. We heard him on the radio: "We're hit. We've been damaged." We watched them fly off in the direction of Thailand.

We came around for one more pass, which was a mistake. It was always a mistake to make more than one pass. The fighter pilots had a saying, "One pass, haul ass!" We knew our chances of being hit increased with every new pass over the target, but we came back.

We were running down the valley again at 500 knots, and we take a hit in the stabulator. The F-4 has a stabulator, a slab in the back that controls the pitch of the aircraft. An antiaircraft shell had exploded right beneath us. The aircraft pitched straight up! We pulled 8-1/2 G's with the first pitch. If we had pitched down, we would have been dead. The force of the explosion caused us to pitch over and back, a slapping up-and-down motion in the air. We were out of control. We both grabbed the stick and froze it. That's the procedure. Here we were running this valley, pitching up and down. I could see the ground when we pitched down, and I could see the ridge when we pitched up. I saw that we were heading right for the wall at the end of the valley. The pitching motion dampened, and we both pulled back on the stick as hard as we could. We came to the ridge, and there was ground all around us. There was an instant's pause—I remembered wondering what it would be like to smash into a wall at 500 knots—and then the ridge just shot away from us and we were in the light of the sky.

Sole Survivor

Billy Walkabout
Tahlequah . . . Phu Bai, 1967–68
Ranger Team Leader, 101st Airborne Division

It's not good for me to be alone now. Even when I sleep, I need to know that someone is nearby. Or I turn the TV on or leave a light on somewhere.

They gave us a job to find an NVA colonel. He was an important dude. He was I Corps commander. He had pulled off Giap's plan for Tet. Hue, Khe Sanh, Dong Ha—he'd been involved in all of that. We were to kill him and get whatever information he had on him.

Since it was going to be a big deal, we combined two six-man teams. My team had been in a lot of shit, but this other team had only blown ambushes. They had killed a lot of gooks, but it's one thing to initiate contact where you blow claymores and spray the area, and it's one hell of another thing when you're getting shot at. This other team hadn't ever been shot at.

We were dropped in at daybreak. In elephant grass. We moved out on a well-traveled trail. Found sleeping bunkers beside the trail. We moved to a little knoll on the map where the man was supposed to be, and bingo! there he was.

Usually Intelligence is not that accurate. They'd tell you a lot of what you're supposed to find on a mission, then you get out there and it's something completely different. The scary thing about this mission was that everything Intelligence had told us was right. The gooks were exactly where they were supposed to be in the numbers they were supposed to be, and there was the colonel. It was too right.

We pulled back a little bit and talked over what we wanted to do. There were gooks everywhere: on top of bunkers, in bunkers, smoking cigarettes, bullshittin'. There were so many gooks it was unbelievable. That night they had flashlights and burned camp fires. We lay in the bush outside their complex and listened to them making noise. Man, they weren't afraid of nothin'. They didn't give a shit who heard them.

We took a vote. We looked hard at each other. I said, "There's probably too many of them, but the way I see it, we got two choices: either do it and get the hell out or we call it off." Everyone said, "Let's do it."

Seven o'clock the next morning, the colonel and his eleven-man entourage move out of the camp. Just like Intelligence told us. There were the eleven-man cadre and a nurse. They said we could be sure it was the colonel if he had two American .45s.

We were off the trail as they came down. I told the other TL to let the point man through and we would trigger the ambush and then pop the point man. We blew the ambush and killed everybody, but the point man got away. Y'know, we just looked away and he was gone.

We hurried into the mess on the trail and stripped the colonel. He had a satchel with nothing but important-looking documents and information. We stripped all the bodies in a hurry. There were gooks, a lot of gooks, heading our way from the bunkers. We knew we had to didi mau the area.

One of the guys from the other team, Contraras, gets in my face and says, "Let me walk point, let me walk point." Now I usually walk point, but I didn't have time to argue. I said, "Get your ass up there."

We're moving our asses and calling for extraction. Contraras takes about six steps and he lights up like a Christmas tree. He must have taken about fifteen hits from an AK. I drag him back, and we're yelling into the phone for immediate medevac.

I pulled us back and up the knoll. At least we had commanding terrain. The gooks surrounded us in a hurry. Then they assaulted us. A full assault, up a hill! I'd been surrounded before, but when gooks come up a hill they mean business. It was thick on the side of that hill with tanglefoot and wait-a-minute vines and shit. It gave them good cover until they were right on us.

We put out fire and pushed them back. We tossed grenades down the hill at them, trying to get air bursts. No response from medevac, gunships. Artillery a big zero. We asked for a reaction company. They said we'd get one, but nothing yet. Since we had to move fast, we didn't carry that much ammo. We only had two days' food. The gooks kept coming and we were running out of ammo. We rolled grenades and ran down the hill and grabbed enemy weapons and used them. We took our claymores, put in fifteen-second delays, and threw them down the hill like great big grenades.

A firefight is instant insanity. Every emotion is running overtime. You live so much in such a short time. You age twenty years. Scared? Yeah. It's something you remember forever, someone pulling a trigger on you. They say war is hell, but contact is a sonofabitch.

We started conserving ammunition. We quit throwing grenades. A guy got shot through the top of the shoulder, so we knew now they had snipers in the trees. We were tucked in together on that little knoll waiting for a big rush, and some gooks got close enough to the top on a blind side to push up a claymore the size of a deuce-'n'-a-half wheel. When it went off, that was the last thing I heard. It took out everybody. I was bleeding from my nose, eyes, and ears. My closest buddy was dead. I talked to him. He shook his head and died. Contraras died. Both of Bacon's legs were blown off. I tried to give him heart massage. One guy had both arms blown off. I gave him mouth-to-mouth until he threw up blood in my face. Frank's chest was blown open. Cox was hit in the back and then in the stomach by an AK. Lender lost both legs and his back was blown to hell.

Now I got four men instantly dead, seven others dying they're hurt so bad. I'm wounded. I can't hear. I'm yelling into the radio for medevacs and I don't even know if they're on. I just yelled into the phone, "TL one-three is down. WIA. Four KIA. Seven WIA, critical." There is no one left standing but me.

It's one o'clock. I'm waiting for artillery, gunships,

anything. No medevacs, and I'm watching my people die. I start moving around our pitiful little perimeter, firing from all positions so the gooks won't know it's just one guy. I wait for another assault, but they start coming up sneaky. They wanted the colonel's papers back. Well, if they would have come all at once they would have had me.

At three o'clock, no reaction company, but artillery shells started landing and a medevac came. Venable died before they got there, but we got out Cox, Lender, and another guy hit worse. I ran around putting them on the jungle penetrator while the chopper hovered.

At five-thirty artillery was doing some good, but people were still coming up at me. Bullets were coming up at me. It had been a long day. I'd been lying on that stinking hill for hours waiting for the government to decide what to do, watching men die. Why did they take so long? I'm just an Indian boy from Oklahoma. What do I know about politics? I just know they didn't come.

Finally the Blues came, and my own company. Of course they are hit themselves and another fight breaks out. They get to us, and they have a medevac for me. I ain't going. Not till the men go. You don't leave your dead. You just don't. Even if they are dead, I am still in charge of them.

They got me off that knoll at seven o'clock. Twelve hours. They flew me to Phu Bai. The first sergeant was there waiting for me. Other people ganged around. There was a guy in a white dress shirt. They took me in this room. A doctor came over with a needle. The guy in the white shirt waved his finger. No anesthetic. This is headquarters. They want to hear the story.

There was a lot of brass. An ARVN officer, this Company man. They start firing questions at me. I can only imagine what they're asking me, since I can't hear yet. "What happened? Did you get the colonel? How many? Are you sure it was the colonel?" I still had the rucksack with all the paper. I opened it up and turned it over and let the two .45s fall out. I can't hear what they're saying, but they are happy. They slap me on the back.

The next day there was a big ceremony. The general gave me a DSC and said to me, "You're the bravest man I ever knew." He had to get real close to my ear. Then he said, "This medal should have been the Medal of Honor, but we downgraded it since you aren't dead." Shit.

It all happened on the twentieth of November. Even today I can't sleep on the night of the nineteenth. I dread it coming. I still see that hill. When they were through with me and I could go back to the barracks, I was alone. The barracks held two teams, and they were all gone. I turned on a light and lay down.

The Sixth Of June

Jim Howarth
Holdenville . . . Tay Ninh, 1968–69
Infantryman, Twenty-fifth Infantry Division

I can remember as a kid playing army. My dad served in the Forty-fifth Infantry Division, and I can remember watching him get dressed for drill. In my generation, if your country called, you went. After I graduated from college in 1967, I checked with my draft board because as I was looking for work, they were always asking my draft status. At the draft board in Holdenville they told me I was due for either June or July, so I joined the Army.

I got orders for Vietnam. I guess I expected it. I knew it was coming, but it was still a shock. In my company roster, 50 percent went to Korea, 50 percent went to Vietnam. It looked like *H* was the dividing line.

Mary Jane and I had been discussing marriage. "I'm going to leave this to you," I told her. "You know I might be killed." She said, "I'd rather be married to you for thirty days than not have you at all." It was nice to go over married, but it was very painful also. We discussed the reality of my being killed or wounded. We elected not to try to have children right away.

I was very afraid, fearful of the unknown. Saying the good-byes was hard. We went to Holdenville. I was very careful not to show too much emotion around my mother, attempt to not hurt her or make things worse. My dad's comments were (he'd been in World War II and Korea): "You've been trained and trained well. Do what they've taught you, and you'll be all right." Visiting Mary Jane's parents and saying good-bye was tough. I remember her mother asking me if I felt like a knight in armor. I wasn't yet that confident. It was the night I had to go out to the airplane. Mary Jane and I sat there holding hands; it was hard to think of something to say. We looked out the window into the dark. Then the plane came up and I kept thinking, "Just go away."

Once I got on the plane, it was kind of a relief. I'm going, I'm moving. My time has started. The flight from Washington to Nam was a faked lightness, playing grab-ass, telling jokes, laughing, as if the jokes would take away the dreaded unknown that lay ahead. Then Cam Ranh Bay. Landing, I was very afraid. The heat, the sauna-like heat. Overwhelming. Like walking into a wall of heat and humidity. And the smell. The odor of Vietnam. Sometimes I can still smell that odor. In-country several months we flew over this area where a large number of enemy had been killed, and you could smell the death even flying over the countryside in choppers.

That first night, it was after midnight, maybe two in the morning, and the heat even then was overwhelming. They hurried us into a big hangar, then onto buses with cages on the windows. They told us later the wire was to keep grenades from being tossed in the windows. They hustled us from place to place, moving us, processing us. And at each stop, I thought, "Now they'll let us sleep." But no: there is the right way, the wrong way, and there is the army way.

Tired, exhausted, twenty hours or more without sleep, we filled sandbags all day long. No shower, no shave, no bed. That night was the first sleep we'd gotten. You could hear the artillery rumbling in the mountains, and I remember laying there and wondering if there was anybody out there those shells were landing on. I cried a little that night. There was the reality that I was a long way from home, I might die, and I might have to kill someone.

They scattered all of us on that plane all over Vietnam. I got orders for the Twenty-fifth. Cu Chi. Then to Tay Ninh. We went through a little five-day orientation. Learned about booby traps, a lot of good stuff but mostly letting you get used to the climate. Other good info: don't drink the Cokes, all the pictures of the social diseases. All that information: treat the Vietnamese with respect, Geneva Convention rules, you are a representative of the United States, all that. One thing that really stuck in my head was the day we went down and filled out the card saying what we wanted as far as notification of family in case we were wounded. Boy, that was a cold slap in the face.

I carried a deck of cards all through Vietnam. Fifty-two. I sent a card a week home to Mary Jane. That was my short-time thing.

When I went for my weapon, I was expecting an M-16, but they handed me this funny-looking thing. I vaguely remembered firing it once in training. M-79. Wait a minute! Sergeant said, "We need a grenadier." "Hey, I haven't been trained with this thing. What the hell do I do with it?" The guy said, "Okay, listen. It's light—what he didn't tell me was the weight of the rounds, especially when you stuff an engineer's bag full—it's easy to clean, and unless it's an emergency, the grenadier doesn't have to walk point." Well, I knew about walking point, so I said, "Okay, I'll take it." I walked point a few times anyway. Not fun.

We got orders we were going to be a blocking force on an operation against an NVA unit, so we started humping. We could hear in the distance a great deal of firing, but we were going to be a blocking force, so it was okay. Soon as we get there, though, we find out we're going to be an additional assault force. We didn't find out until later just how big an operation this thing was. It wasn't major, but it was big. A cav and an armor unit was next to us.

My first firefight lasted all day long. It started early in the morning. My water was gone by midmorning, my lips bled. It was strange and confusing. We were on line, assaulting. They said shoot at the bunkers, so I started popping rounds. Things were exploding. I even had thoughts of "Wow! this is neat, this is war! Exciting." And my God, it was. It was a high. Every sense was alive. It was as if I could sense all in every pore.

But I'd look around and see GIs fall. That wasn't me, though. I said, "I won't get hit." A magic about me. No one was going to shoot through this magic wall around me. But the thought came: here I am standing, and this enemy is in the ground, and they're eventually going to shoot me. I fought the fear, the panic I felt. They are. A debate going on in my mind all the time I was popping rounds. Then it was pull back, advance, pull back, advance. Artillery, jet strikes, shrapnel from our own guns hitting us. All day long.

The deep fear didn't strike until that night, when it was over, and then I got the shakes. I had loose bowels. I felt bad about that until I heard that even some of the old-timers had them, too.

The next day was my birthday. I spent my birthday sweeping the area searching bodies. I came upon a dead NVA. I searched his body. I still have a North Vietnamese stamp I took from him. He had a diary, which I had to turn

in to Intelligence. The last page of the diary had the most
beautiful drawing of a peace dove with the olive branch. I
realized this guy had been a human. With feelings. I found
his wallet. A picture. There was a picture of a woman and
two kids. I said, "Jesus!"

The body searching was sickening. I couldn't look at the
dead men. I was afraid to touch them, the feeling they
had. Then I just shut down. I became numb to it. So I
could get through without being laughed at, I thought. I
didn't want to vomit. I didn't think about it. I made myself
not think about the dead enemy as humans, as guys who
used to think about wives, used to think about kids. I
fought off flashes of myself lying down there dead. What
would I look like dead? Would my mouth be left hanging
open? Would my eyes be open staring up at the sun? Would
I swell up, be left lying there? I saw head wounds, chest
wounds, arms and legs just hanging on to the body by a
sliver of muscle. It was scary, but I made myself go
through it. Protective numbness.

My shutdown came early. We had a prisoner, a VC
suspect. I was sitting nearby, either reading or writing a
letter from home or to home. I remembered this because I
carried a picture of our wedding inside my helmet, and I
had this out while I was writing. At the same time, I was
watching this guy being interrogated by the South Vietnamese. They were rough, beating him around. A .45 to
his head, beating him and kicking him, asking him questions. The guy was crying, bleeding, and I was just writing
a letter. I turned up and watched, like in a trance, and all
of a sudden this .45 went off, and I saw this head turn into
a pink mist, chips of bone, pieces of skin, hair. And I
went back to writing the letter, just as if that were the
normal daily event or job: pick up the groceries, wash the
car, blow someone's head away. We moved out, and I

looked at the guy lying there, with his head blown open, and I remember thinking about the college textbooks. Yeah, it really looks like that. There's the gray matter and all that. Except this one was all messed up. It was a curiosity to me. A sergeant picked up a machete and drove it into the dead guy's head. This bothered me. Funny. The other didn't, but this did. The sergeant was warped. He stuck a card in the dead man's face. Again, that was okay somehow, but not the machete to the head.

I have two birthdays: my official birthday and my spiritual birthday. June 6, 1968, is my spiritual birthday. We were going out on an easy operation. I even took a paperback with me.

We knew something was wrong before we landed. It was a hot LZ. My company went one way and the other company the other way across the road. It was a hot LZ. As we were landing the door gunner yelled at us to put on our gas masks. I didn't even know if mine worked. Where did the gas come from? We landed hard. I jumped out one side with another guy. Mass confusion, noise, limited vision with gas masks on. Didn't even know where the shooting was coming from. All of a sudden I had this strong feeling to get down fast. I just dropped on the road—we'd had to land single file on this narrow road. As I was on my way to the ground, I heard this dull crunching noise. I looked over my shoulder and saw the tail boom of the ship I was on go right over me. Had I been standing, I would have been decapitated. The ship behind mine had attempted to lift off too soon and the main rotor hit the rear rotor of the chopper I had been on. All crew members jumped out, and they became grunts for a while.

Out of the chaos, some sort of organization occurred. I remember lying in this ditch; next to me was the crew of the chopper. The chopper kept making this noise, the sound as one begins to rev up. Then a splashing noise as if water were dropping on a hot plate. The crew were concerned about some switch on something left on that might cause the ship to explode. Great! Will I die in this explosion or by Charlie? Finally the door gunner popped up, ran to the ship, and hit the switch. The noise stopped. Some relief, except for the enemy across the road, unseen but shooting away.

As we were landing, several men were wounded even before we hit ground. They had a medevac en route so we had to begin to clear the area, provide some security. One company went one way, my company, Alpha Company, went another. All hell broke loose. We lost radio contact. The other company was hit bad, killed or wounded, completely wiped out across the road. We started going over, dragging back the dead and wounded. Every time we crossed we took a casualty or a KIA.

At some point that afternoon I realized I was going to die that day. June 6 would be my last day on this earth. I was very afraid. I had been across the road four times, and I was getting ready to go again. I had dragged back guys that were dead, guys that were hit bad. One guy was hit in the groin and he was being loaded on the medevac and the NVA hit the medevac with an RPG. It killed the ship. I think the crew made it out alive. And the wounded, I guess, just gave up and died. I got real angry, and I didn't care. I wanted to kill as many as I could. I was in a daze. I said a prayer. I grew up in the church. The prayer was real simple: "Today's it. Take care of the people back home." And at that time I gave up thinking about me and I started thinking about Mary Jane and my parents and how they'd take it because I figured we were going to be wiped out. They would overrun us at any time. A unit kept trying to come in down the road to help us, but they kept getting ambushed every time they tried. Units of the Twenty-fifth, and I think even units of the 101st, tried, but they couldn't get to us.

When I said that prayer, I was still afraid, but a certain amount of peace came over me. Almost like I'm dead and now I'm just going through the motions. I don't know how to describe the feeling. Peace doesn't really describe it. Almost like on a very hot day and suddenly you pass onto a cool mountaintop, that kind of feeling. A washing over, a cleansing. Peaceful, like I was in a dream. I was still afraid. I wanted to do what I could to stay alive, but I'm already dead, mixed with that peace. I spent the rest of that afternoon as if I wasn't there, like in a dream.

That night we got separated from the rest of the unit. A cherry lost eye contact with the man in front of him. Four of us were lost. There were thirty-six hours of extreme fear. I knew I was dead.

Death was too close to me at that time. I remember we ran out of body bags and the bodies were lined up on the ground, poncho liners covering the dead, the tags on the toes. I remember guys dying that day among us and them passing gas as they died. The smell of blood, the smell of dead guys already starting to rot, and the smell of guys passing gas as they died. Some died wetting their pants. Other guys lying in trenches peeing out of fear. You couldn't stand up, so you just did it in your pants. You didn't think anything of it.

I went by one guy on a stretcher in a pool of blood under his head, and he looked up at me and I was embarrassed. I didn't know what to say to him. I couldn't comfort him. I just looked at him and walked on.

I had the runs the next day from fear. My body took over. It was days after that area was secure and I still had that extreme feeling of fear and dread deep inside me. I was still having occasional diarrhea. They thought I had a bug so they sent me to a medical unit. Two days they had me there and couldn't find a bug. It was psychological, I guess.

Afterward I remembered that feeling of peace I had that day, and it was a good feeling. It wasn't like coming home, but it was good. I learned a lot about myself that day.

Watching From the Sea

Greg Motto
Claremore . . . Gulf of Tonkin, 1961–62, 1967–68
Machinist's Mate, First Class, USS **Long Beach**

I recall the cabin fever. We were out there in the gulf for five months at a time, going in five-mile squares at five knots. Day after day, square after square. The boredom was broken in the morning and evening by being called to General quarters. Battle stations.

I remember fighting a below-decks fire next to our nuclear-missile storage. I remember listening to the radios and the noises of war. But mostly I remember huge chunks of nothingness divided twice daily, periods of intense activity followed by time for contemplation. Is this the time we'll be blown out of existence? Or do the same to someone else? This span of time after the necessities of battle preparedness had been done gave us all time to think about what could come next. Fear is too mild a word for what I felt most of these times. Scared shitless is a little closer to the truth.

I was a lifer until that last tour.

I was part of a naval force fifteen miles off the coast, knowing our ground troops were being hit. We could watch the evening sky and see the firefights. We had to watch the MIGs screaming at us out of Haiphong. We couldn't fire at them; Washington wouldn't let us. Frustration. More frustration. Boredom. Raw-edged nerves.

We were coordinating all this destruction, and what were we accomplishing? I have asked myself this question countless times since, and I still don't have an answer.

Ambush

Jim Yearout
Harrah . . . Mekong Delta, 1971–72
Platoon Leader, Kit Carson Scouts

We'd gone into an area around My Tho, knowing that there was a sizable Viet Cong unit around. We went in there, as usual, as an intelligence-gathering unit rather than purely combat. But it didn't always work out that way. This time we were in for a surprise.

We set up an L-shaped ambush just in case we had to fight. We set our claymores out in front of us along the dike there, and about three in the morning a VC unit started coming in. At first there were sixty-five or seventy of them, but it ended up being about two companies of VC. There were only fifteen of us! Hah, that's funny now, but at the time I thought there was no way we were going to get out of there.

I was the platoon leader, the only American, but I felt secure with these guys—as safe as you can feel in combat, that is. We worked with the ARVN almost entirely, though we were supported by American artillery and gunships. Usually we were inserted in the field by going out with a large ARVN unit and then dropping out of the line and going on our own. We were sneaky. My scouts were good, tough. They knew VC tactics because they'd all been Viet Cong at one time. We recruited them that way. We took men whose family had members killed by the VC. By the time they came over to us, they were motivated to kill Communists. They respected me. I never felt they would turn me over to the Communists.

They would send us in on unusual missions. Once there were intelligence reports that there was a salt-and-pepper team working in the area. There had been numerous sightings of two GIs, deserters or defectors, working with the Viet Cong as snipers. We didn't find any signs of them, but we kept hearing more about them.

This time outside My Tho, this unit came through and we ambushed them. I had two machine guns at the end of the L, and they opened up. When the VC turned and ran our way, we blew the claymores. We wiped the dike with them. But what we didn't know was there was that other company coming in behind them. We had to call in the gunships to help get us out; we had no choice. Two gunships came in and literally peeled the VC off our backs until we could get out of the area.

Builders In the Jungle

Melvin Wren
Bethel . . . Bong Song, 1967–68
First Sergeant, Thirty-fifth Combat Engineers

Sometimes we would have to be the first into an area, ahead of the infantry. As combat engineers, we were responsible for our own security. Mainly we would be ambushed on roads or at the job sites. We'd have to leave equipment out at night, and the VC would booby-trap it. By a village we left some lumber stacked outside, and somebody got to it. Next morning my men started working with it, and it exploded. We had to fish 'em out of the river where they'd jumped to get the white phosphorus off of them. We'd have serious ambushes where we'd lose two or three men at a time. Frustrating as hell 'cause we couldn't go after them. We just defended ourselves at that particular point. Sure, we could call in planes and artillery, but hell, the enemy were gone by the time help came.

One of the saddest things—needless things—happened in my unit. We were sitting up on Bong Son, sitting on top of the hill. It got real hot at night up there. We had guards out front. At two o'clock in the morning I heard a rifle shot and went out to check. This one guard was out on what we called the front gate, up on a bunker. He got up

on the bunker where he could get some air, a little breeze.
Well, his buddy went out to visit him. He was gonna scare
him, I guess, 'cause he snuck up behind him. Kid turned
around and shot his buddy right between the eyes with an M-14.

PART THREE

The Edge Of the World

Music

David Samples
Sapulpa . . . Dong Ha, 1966–67
Seabee, U.S. Navy Mobile Construction

Music was important to the Nam experience. It was everywhere. It had a message, and to a lot of us it came loud
and clear. WAR! / Good God / What is it good for? /
Absolutely nothin'! / All the time we were caught up
in war.

It was a war supposedly to win the hearts and minds of
the people. Only thing, these people were as different from
us as cave people to space men. We didn't understand
them. We didn't trust them. They envied our materialistic
world or thought they did. And they hated what we did to
them and theirs. And we did plenty. We made prostitutes
out of their women and whored their government. We turned
their ancestral villages into free-fire zones. We helped
make Viet Cong out of peasant boys and girls. We turned
a farming society into a refugee society in order to
control the enemy. I think we just helped spread death
and desolation. I don't think we won too many hearts and
minds.

The cause started out a good one, but too many chefs
spoil the pot, isn't it? Between the politicians and the
generals, hawks and doves, war profiteers and industry,
somehow we lost track of the objective. The teen-age

soldiers got old beyond their years and realized survival was the only goal. Rightly so. The American fighting man, along with the Vietnamese peasant, became the butt of the worst joke of the century. A joke that killed a lot of people, Vietnamese and American. Maimed a lot of people, left them physically and mentally hurt, doomed to suffer in a country that now finds shame in them, a reminder of the joke. It split our nation as badly as the Civil War.

Anytime I hear the Bee Gees sing, "I started a joke that started the whole world laughing," I think of the war. We lived in a rock-and-roll world, our generation did. Our generation was caught up in the music, and when the war came along it was only natural that the music joined in. In the Nam we changed old tunes slightly to our way of thinking. Jerry Lee Lewis:

> You shake my nerves and you rattle my brain.
> Too much WAR makes a man insane.
> You broke my will,
> But what a thrill!
> Goodness gracious great balls of fire.

We got falling-down drunk and higher than the war to rock and roll. I can still remember so many nights spent drunk, listening to Iron Butterfly's "In-a-gadda-da-vida" punctuated by incoming rounds and men who were wounded and dying, crying, and screaming. So we just changed the words: "In the Garden of Eden." Some joke, but we laughed. We laughed at everything. Laughter was a cover-up; it was laugh or cry. And like the saying goes: If you cry, you cry alone; laugh and the world laughs with you. So we laughed. It was cruel laughter sometimes. I still laugh, but it is to hide my tears. I remember laughing when things were bad, and we would laugh until we were limp. It was like we were laugh addicted, and we just stared at each other. Hey, turn up the music and pass the beer, and maybe we'll make it through the night.

If the music hadn't been written at the time we were in Vietnam, it came out later to help bring us nightmares and guilt. Guilt for the dead. For the ruined forests. The ruined society. The children. Oh, the children. I had to watch a ten-year-old girl die from one of our mistakes. They were just playing, her brothers and sisters, and she was killed. Her eyes. Their eyes. Number Ten, GI.

Those poor people. They didn't want Communism or democracy. They wanted to be left alone to work their rice paddies, their farms. Between us and the Commies, we destroyed and desolated their homes. We killed their families, hearts, and minds.

Killing Monkeys
And Choosing Between
Bad and Worse

Robert Kirk
Oklahoma City . . . Danang, 1969–70
F-4 Fighter Pilot, 480th Tactical Fighter Squadron

We killed a lot of monkeys. Some missions just weren't worth flying. Some, however, were very important. The war represented one of the hardest years of my life. There was fear. There was the ethics of the whole thing. There were profound moral decisions to be made.

I wasn't a hero. So much of what I did was out of duty. On my tour I flew 197 combat missions in the F-4. For me they more or less fit into two categories: the worthless jobs, the bombing runs on trails, or shooting monkeys, and the important jobs, helping friendly ground troops. We would scramble, work out of the alert shack in twelve-hour shifts, fly in support of ground troops in contact. These were important missions! That's the way we felt. When we knew there were troops in trouble, there was absolutely no question about us coming to help. We felt good about these missions; these were the missions worth flying.

Serving in the military during a war meant the possibility of killing. This was not something I wanted to do, but I was torn between conscience and obligation and responsibility. I didn't understand what was happening in my life. It was like my life was out of control. Some of my friends did things to stay out of the war. There were also the choices of Canada and Sweden, but I couldn't make those choices. There was the feeling that my country had given me something. I had to give something back.

I was already out of college and teaching school in Moore. I went before the draft board believing I had a legitimate request for deferment. I was a full-time science teacher in the public schools and going to graduate school full time in the evenings. I was reclassified 1-A. I thought it was a mistake. I was told I could appeal to my draft board. I decided to appeal. I'll never forget standing before those old men. They didn't say one word to me as I presented my case. Not one word. I had a bad feeling about it all. A lady took me into the room with the men, and when I was through she took me out of the room. She did all the talking for the men. I held out no hope at all when I heard another lady telling this very young-looking eighteen-year-old black kid whom I was sitting with and who couldn't read or write say, "Just put your mark right here." There was no doubt where he was headed.

What to do? I was torn. There were no good choices. It was like deciding between bad and worse. Now I can joke about it. They tried to draft me for two years, but I showed them: I joined for five!

Add to all this indecision, conscience, and feelings of obligation a personal tragedy on my way to Vietnam. My father died while I was in the Philippines for survival training. I went back to the States again. Saying good-bye to my wife and family had been unbelievably hard, and now I had to come back to be with my family in more grief. On the flight home, my thoughts were on my father.

I wrote a poem about him. My father's death was the hardest thing. I almost felt I couldn't work through it.

The first thing I saw on the pilots' scheduling board at my squadron in Danang were small parachutes, signs beside some of the names on the board. I asked what they meant. I was told, "Those are the guys who've been shot down." There were several on the board. I found out one of the names was of a friend of mine, a guy I took F-4 training with. That was a real shock. He had been picked up by the helicopters and was alive. I remembered I wanted to talk with him, but I never was able to see him.

I felt like a gladiator. They put us in module barracks. We had air conditioning, steaks on ice. Officers' club, movies, ice cream. But every day, essentially, we all knew we were going to have to do things that might get us killed. Nobody got shot at more than the fighter pilot. The difference is: if you don't get hit, it doesn't exist, it's not happening; but if you do get hit, you're probably dead or in prison. There was a lot of fear, and it was strongest just before you went in. But once your run started, you were too busy; there were just so many things to do you didn't have time for fear.

Soon for me the war came down to three important truths. First, make it back home. Second, put it all out on the line only if friendly troops needed help or your friends were in trouble. Third, there were a lot of things in Vietnam not worth doing.

Choices. It came down to making choices. The whole war experience was very personal. I was a patriot, I loved my country, I would fight. I was a Christian, I believed the Bible, I believed it wrong to kill, how could I kill? More and more I believed it was all politics and economics. Some things just didn't add up. The war machine got going and it couldn't be stopped, and as it rolled on and I became part of it, I felt betrayed.

Absurd. I received a Distinguished Flying Cross. Someone put me in for it. I wasn't even sure then what mission it was for! The absurdity of it all hit me hardest one in-country mission. We made our runs with 500-pound high-drag bombs, very accurate. The forward air controller called our runs. We were hitting a suspected troop concentration in a bunker complex. We had made several runs when the FAC told us an old man had walked out of one of the bunkers and was sitting on a log. He had staggered out of a bunker into full view, just sitting there (my guess dying), with all this destruction around him. I don't know what was going through his mind, but I felt sorrow for him.

The FAC came back on the radio and was going crazy. He was shouting, "Kill him, kill him!" Our wingman made a run at the old man with a 20-mm cannon. He opened up and somehow missed him. What must the old man be thinking? He's just trying to die, and here are these crazies risking a two-million-dollar aircraft and two pilots to kill an old man. It was ludicrous. The FAC screamed again, "You missed! Kill him, kill him!" It was madness. I came on the radio and said, "Let's go home."

In The Shadow Of the Mountain

J.D. Maples
Muskogee . . . Firebase Bear Cat, 1969–70
Machinegunner, Twenty-fifth Infantry Division

First day we're saddling up and they hand me the 60. I say, "No way I'm carrying that heavy thing." "Yeah, you got to. You're big and stout, you can handle it." I told them, "I'm not going to. I want an M-16." "Fine," they said, "you walk point." It was three or four klicks of hard humping to the forward firebase. I said "Where's the 60?"

Our sister company was in trouble on the side of Nui Ba Dinh, a huge mountain. They told us to get ready; we were going in to help them.

We landed and made our way up the side of that mountain, and it was tough going. We dug and tried to sleep. We dug these three-man holes. You know you don't ever go to sleep completely out there. It's that light, nervous sleep. Every nerve on edge.

Three in the morning we hear thump, thump, thump. They are walking the mortars in on us. We had dug the holes before we set up for the night, and everybody started jumping for the holes. It was so dark you couldn't see anything. Six men jumped into our three-man hole. There was a great crash and everything went white. I was scared. I felt this wet stuff trickle down my face. I just knew I was hit. There were guys on top of me in the hole. There just wasn't room for that many. I realized the wet stuff was brains and blood. At first I thought it was mine till I looked above me and saw one guy with the top of his head gone, and the other had holes in his chest, and his blood bubbled in the holes.

I'm a big guy, but I got weak and lost down to 142 pounds. One night I fell asleep on watch. I shit my pants, and I remember thinking, "I'm gonna die." I'd always heard that's the last thing to go before you die. I was so thirsty I was sneaking away, crawling into bomb craters and drinking that rotten water. I got to where I couldn't eat C rations. I learned to speak Vietnamese enough that I could get their food. But I stopped that after mamasan fed me rat stew.

We went sixty-three days without seeing the rear area. My lieutenant, a guy by the name of Lope, and I got along good. We were friends. We got to be good soldiers in the jungle. We could count on each other. We were staying alive.

They sent us a new captain. The captains rotated a lot, and it seemed we were always getting new ones. This guy was sorry; he got us lost. Lope and I looked up and here comes the captain with his RTO and his whole damn entourage doubling back, coming right up to us, making a cluster. He wanted to talk about it. Now everybody knows you don't cluster up in the jungle: one shell gets all of you. I'm thinking, "This ain't worth a damn," when over behind a berm two gooks set off a command-detonated ambush. It was a 105 round, and the way they had it rigged it did a lot of damage. Guys were laying everywhere, but I went to Lope. Half his neck was blown away, his biceps were torn open, his leg muscles were shredded.

There was so much blood. I couldn't stop the blood. I put my hands one place, but then I'd think, "no, put them here." I felt him getting cold.

There were snipers in a hedgerow. We couldn't get to them. We moved on and I heard a single crack, that unmistakable crack an AK makes. A big guy from Arkansas was walking close to me. That one round picked him up off the ground and carried him ten feet and slammed him up against a tree. I went down, but instead of staying down, I had an ammo bearer hook his rounds onto my starter belt. I don't know what was going on in my head. I was tired of it, sick of guys dying. I was mad, I was thinking of everything, I was thinking of nothing at all. I started running at the hedgerow, firing the 60 like an M-16. There was screaming, but I don't know if it was from my buddies or from me. The snipers couldn't shoot because I kept firing one long burst and they couldn't raise their heads. I only saw my rounds hit one guy, but they were all dead. The one I saw, he was cut almost in two, but he was still alive. Son, our Kit Carson Scout, followed me in there. He started kicking this guy and shouting at him in Vietnamese. Son fired some more rounds in him. Then a crazy thing happened: I didn't want this guy to die. He was torn up so bad and looking up at me scared, knowing he was dying. I started crying and trying to help this guy I'd killed. I told Son, "C'mon, we gotta do something for him," and Son looked at me like I was nuts. He shook his head. The guy was finished, couldn't I see? I didn't want this man to die. Son just walked off and left me there.

They'd been trying for a long time to get me off the line, to take a rear job before I went home. I wouldn't do it. After this, I knew it was time for me to get out.

Russian Guns

Terry Dyke
Aydelotte . . . Pleiku, 1967–68
Reconnaissance Pilot, 219th Aviation Company

We came around very low, and I'm looking right at this guy behind a .50-cal. He's smiling, like, "I got you." One tracer round came through my windshield. I know this sounds crazy, but I think I dodged it. My plane had self-sealing, rubber-lined tanks, but I was still afraid of it exploding. I had a new observer in the back, and this flipped him out. He let go from both ends. What a mess in the back seat. No time to worry about my rolling stomach.

Someone had reported sighting NVA with a pair of Russian field guns, and we had found them. And the .50-cal had found us. When we took the round, I banked the plane to the left with the stick and at the same time kicked the rudder to the right. This is cross-control; you don't do it because it's very dangerous, but we were caught low in the open and I had to try something. I thought I was going down. I lowered the nose to keep from stalling.

We went low into a bunch of NVA. They're all there, swarming, popping at us with AKs and the .50. There were the two big guns Intelligence was looking for right in the middle of them. A round came through the plane between me and the observer. He started screaming, "It's coming through the sides!'' We got out of there and called in coordinates so they could fire on them.

The guns were destroyed, and in the debriefing I reported that the guns weren't Communist at all; they were just a pair of captured American 105s, but they didn't listen. They wanted something political. The next day in the papers: ''Russ Guns Knocked Out.''

Disease In Saigon

Jack Welsh
Oklahoma City . . . Can Tho, 1967–68
Physician, Volunteer Physicians for Vietnam Program

Dr. Joel Brown, a former Special Forces, former Walter Reed team member who was part of our University of Oklahoma medical-school faculty in Saigon, once said that the diseases in Vietnam were not exotic but were just the common everyday diseases present in a Third World country. They certainly were not the ones seen in Oklahoma or elsewhere in the United States! Everyone who came over for short periods to help with the teaching at the medical school was exhorted to review his old tropical-medicine textbooks. Having been in the Delta, I had already seen many of these infectious diseases among the rural population. However, I did not expect to see them in Saigon when the O.U. College of Medicine assumed an active role in helping the South Vietnamese medical-school faculty in 1969. This was certainly not the case. Disease killed more of the people in the rural and urban areas than the war.

Tuberculosis was everywhere, as was expected, but there was a very good TB hospital staffed by excellent Vietnamese doctors who provided treatment once the diagnosis was made. Dr. Jim Hammersten, head of the College of Medicine at Oklahoma, an internationally known pulmonary specialist, established a very good and productive working relationship with the Vietnamese physicians at the tuberculosis hospital. The lack of good X-ray facilities made it difficult, however, to reach a diagnosis in some cases at Cho Ray, a large, old, rambling multiple-building hospital built by the French and which was at first our main teaching and service hospital. When things broke down, X-rays were dried along with some laundry: outside in the sun.

Acute rheumatic fever, which had become relatively rare in the United States, was common, and the cardiac ravages of the disease were present among many of the children and young adults. Surgical correction was not practical, with the general conditions of the hospitals, and good long-term medical care was almost impossible to achieve. Various American groups got a lot of publicity from flying some of the children back to the States for cardiac surgery. Corrective surgery was the glamour part of the problem but prevention was what was needed, and it was hard to get any support or enthusiasm for a program to prevent the disease and provide help on a larger scale. We tried to teach the need for this approach and the importance of other types of preventive medicine for the people of the country to the medical students.

Typhoid, along with its complication of intestinal perforations, which had been frequent in the Delta, was also present in Saigon. There were always patients with typhoid on the general medical wards and at the infectious-disease hospital, Cho-Quan. I had expected the patients with typhoid to come from the rural areas, but instead most lived in Saigon or Gia Dinh. Three of the Oklahoma medical-school faculty—Drs. Brown, Butler, and Arnold—demonstrated the first Chloramphenical-resistant typhoid in Vietman. How much of this resistance to the antibiotic developed because the typhoid bacterium was just a smart bug or because of the ready availability of antibiotics was not clear. Antibiotics were available at any pharmacy without a prescription, and the package inserts recommended their use for the common cold! A large sign on the Saigon River bank even advertised Typhomycin (Chloramphenical).

Vietnam was the plague capital of the world. In October of 1970 the International Plague Conference was held in Saigon. Dr. Dave Neumann, a graduate of the O.U. medical school who was with the army, presented some of the work he had done on the rat and flea population that carried the disease. Most of the plague was from Cu Chi, which is not far from Saigon. Most of the patients came to Cho-Quan Hospital in Saigon. The doctors who worked at the hospital were Vietnamese and experienced in the diagnosis and treatment of the disease. Some of our people also worked at the hospital a few times a week. Once a mother brought a child who had plague into the hospital and, as was the usual case, stayed with him in his room. Within a few days she developed a plague bubo. To see a bubo develop before your eyes was truly amazing and something very, very few Western doctors in our time have witnessed.

There was a real effort to help the people through improvement of the medical-education system. It was just reaching the point when things were starting to get better when it all went down the tube. The students and young faculty were as good as anywhere in the world. They just needed help, encouragement, understanding, and a push once in a while—like any students.

Water In A Boot

Mark Hatfield
Coweta . . . LZ North English, 1969–70
Paratrooper, 173rd Airborne Division

Hawk teams went out on night patrols and ambushed the gooks when they moved in and out of the villages. We had been out for four nights, humping the hills, not finding anything. This was our last night out, so we were lax. In a cemetery not far from base, we set up an ambush, but it was a half-assed one. We were tired, we hadn't found any gooks in the area, and it was raining. Guys were playin' grab-ass.

A speed trail went right down the middle of the graves, and we set up behind the mounds. You know how the gook graves were, built up in mounds. Good places to hide behind. There was a creek behind us, and we found out later there were some caves up in the hills. But it looked like we weren't going to have any contact, and I was glad of it because we had about ten cherries with us on this patrol. In the morning we'd walk in and have a few days off.

I was humping the 60, and I was so lax I didn't even

have it loaded. I had it and the ammo covered with a ponch 'cause it was raining.

We finally got quieted down. I was on watch in the dark and I heard this noise right behind me. It was a sucking sound, y'know, like water in a boot. I sat up and looked over a headstone at this guy. I was really going to get onto him for making noise when I saw the look on his face. He heard it, too! The gooks were on the move from the caves to the village, and they were coming right through us.

Taking Time For Feelings

Marguerite Giroux
Oklahoma City . . . Bien Hoa, 1965–66
Nurse, Third Surgical Hospital

We did some marvelous things in Vietnam, but we couldn't save them all. It all happened so fast when you were trying to save someone; you couldn't take time for your feelings, you couldn't let it get to you. Nothing could prepare you for the sight of the mangled bodies. Those sights remain vivid.

One night a Marine was brought in, horribly wounded by a grenade. It had blown up in his hands. His face was gone; eyes, nose, mouth, and hands gone; nothing but a bloody hole for his face. We tried to save him, but we couldn't stop the bleeding. He was dying, and despite these incredible wounds he shook his head back and forth like he wanted to live. I wanted to comfort him, but there were no hands to hold, no eyes to see. I begged God to take him.

Rockets

David Mead
Lawton . . . Can Tho, 1968–69
Gunship Pilot, 162nd Assault Helicopter Company

Rockets landed on us in the night, and people were running for cover everywhere. The CO was pissed. He couldn't find the gunnies, who were supposed to be in the air looking for the tubes. The gunship platoon leader was drunk. No way he could fly. I ran smack into the CO. He grabbed me.

"Can you take the gunships up?" he asked.

"Yes, sir," I said quickly.

"Good," he said, "you're the new gunship platoon leader. Now go find those tubes and knock them out!"

I took advantage of an opportunity offered me. I became a gunship pilot in a most unusual way. I had been flying slicks. I had never flown a gunship before. In training, a certain percentage were taken to the firing range with gunships, but I never was. I wanted to try one.

Immediately, I began rounding up the gunship pilots. It took me a while to get the ships in the air because as I would go up to each gunnie, I had to retell the story, explain how I came to be their new platoon leader.

I called a meeting the next day. I knew I would have to earn their respect. I was determined to do it. I was straight with them. I told them I had no experience with gunships but I would learn and learn fast. I knew I had to be honest; they'd see through bullshit. To earn their respect, I knew I would have to learn quickly.

I don't think I ever experienced deep fear flying; there were too many responsibilities. You didn't get a long time to think. I had to monitor five radios, coordinate the gunship formation, watch the slick formation, keep in contact with the C&C ship, and fire the weapons.

I felt comfortable in the cockpit. I was in control. Flying became second nature. What fear I experienced was in being rocketed at two in the morning. I couldn't stand staying down in a bunker. I was paranoid. It was SOP during rocket attacks that each platoon have one man with a shotgun guard the flight line against sappers. I never even told my men about this. I always took that job myself to stay out of a bunker.

An infantry squad was pinned down about two miles from base. They were too near to get help from artillery, and the F-4s were unavailable. We only had one gunship up. The cardinal rule of gunnies was, "Never put in a one-ship strike," but these guys were hurting so I said I would go up.

The sergeant came on the radio and said, "They are fifteen yards in front of us, and we've been here all night."

I told him, "Okay, I'm coming, but I'm by myself so I'll have to get real close."

A bird dog, a forward air controller, was in the area—he

turned out to be a guy I was in flight training with—and he came on the radio and said, "Anything I can do?" Well, these guys are not known for their firepower, but I could take any help I could get. He said, "All I've got is some Willy Pete, some smoke, and an M-16."

He went in first because he was more vulnerable. I covered him. He was really something flying that thing. On his pass, he had the M-16 out the window firing it and tossing out smoke grenades.

If there were troops on the ground, we did everything possible to help them. We just didn't think about not coming in.

Our primary responsibility on a combat assault was the safety of the slicks and the ground troops in them. We gave cover fire as the troops left the slicks and made it to the wood line. We watched to make sure the slicks cleared the LZ, then we went back to base to reload. Then we came back. We would contact the C&C and find out what he wanted us to do. If the troops were in contact, we helped, and if there were dust-offs, we covered them. By the way, any helicopter in the area was a medevac. That's all there was to it. You didn't always wait for a medevac chopper. If someone was hurt, you picked him up whether you were a slick or whatever.

When firing for troops in contact, you pinpointed the area and then went in firing in teams of two gunships or four. You couldn't help being concerned about hitting your own men. It bothered us all. I cringed to think I might get back to base and be told I'd hit one of our ground troops. I'd watch closely as the troops headed for the wood line, and I would be careful to put my rockets safely away from them in the trees.

Once the CO jumped my ass after a combat assault. I

had fired my rockets like I always did, just ahead of our troops, just inside the wood line. He screamed at me, "Don't you know how to fire rockets? I want you firing right on the edge of the wood line!"

The next time out, I watched the troops running for the wood line, then I put my rockets cleanly on the edge of the wood line. It seemed like it was right on top of our men. "If that's where you want 'em, that's where you get 'em," I thought to myself. It seemed like taking too much risk, but I could put the rockets anywhere they thought they belonged. We got back to base, and one of the slick pilots came up to me and flipped me a chunk of shrapnel that had torn through his door window on the LZ. He said to me, "I believe this is yours."

A congressman wanted to see the action. You know, a combat assault. See how it really was, get in the action. So we loaded up the slicks with grunts. The congressman and his entourage were in a separate ship, very high in the sky, waiting for the show to begin. We flew out into the countryside, all these troops and slicks and gunships. At the LZ, artillery blasted the area, jets came in, and then we blew the place all to hell. Nothing left of it.

So the slicks came in and the grunts charged to the wood line like there could possibly be any enemy anywhere in the area. The congressman never got close to the ground, but we did get an attaboy from six thousand feet.

91 Golf

Jim Howarth
Holdenville . . . Tay Ninh, 1968–69
Infantryman, Twenty-fifth Infantry Division

Orders were cut for me to come out of the field and go to Cu Chi. The Twenty-fifth Medical Battalion mental-hygiene section had requested anyone who had gone to college and majored in psychology or had some training in one of the social sciences. They needed some help as a 91 Golf, which was a psychological technician. I was a college graduate with a lot of hours in psychology. They picked me.

At first I had mixed feelings about leaving my unit. At first I felt bad. Why me? Just because I had been to college. But, my buddies were happy for me. They slapped me on the back. I told them, "If you ever get into Cu Chi, look me up and I'll buy you a beer."

Every time a unit was hit, I'd go down and check the KIA and the WIA list. A lot of times, if there were mass casualties, they'd pull us all, and we'd go down and unload Chinooks, carrying stretchers into surgery.

One day I got word my unit was hit. I think it was Thanksgiving week; it might even have been Thanksgiving Day. I went to the KIA book and started looking down the names. I must have gone into shock because I was halfway back to the mental-hygiene section, maybe fifty meters away, and all of a sudden I didn't remember reading that book. I didn't even remember seeing names. That was curious to me. I went back and talked to the clerk. I said, "Let me see that book again."

Names. Guys in my platoon, my squad, guys that I knew. I remember the guys even now. I don't remember their names. Some had nicknames. There was Red, a guy from the Carolinas, uneducated. I loved the guy. He was killed. Another guy, he got a Dear John letter, he was killed. And a lot of other guys I knew were killed. To this day I wonder, if I had been there, would I have been killed too? When Thanksgiving Day comes around, I always wonder.

Stay With That Indian!

Danny Bruner
Broken Arrow . . . Central Highlands, 1968–69
Infantryman, Fourth Infantry Division

Don't put down that I was near a city or a base. I was in the bush, man! For me it was seven straight months of humping, diggin' in, sweating, eating cold food, thirsting, being scared, and fighting. And you couldn't get out for nothin'. Guys too weak to walk were made to stay in the bush. Guys walked around without shirts and with pants rotting off them. I had diarrhea so bad I lost down to 140 pounds. The line of march would have to stop so

I wouldn't shit my pants. You think they let me out for that? Shit, no.

All that time I saw maybe five guys get out of the jungle the right way, the regular way. Everybody else left by being killed or being wounded. I heard of guys coming back to Nam for a second tour. That's crazy. I'll tell you one thing: nobody who came back for a second tour was doing what I was doing. No way. Nobody would take two doses of what I took.

It was hard work. You had to carry so much weight. I carried a ton of water. When you were resupplied, they gave out threes and fours; that means three sodas or four beers. Guys would trade off, and you gorged yourself and threw away what you couldn't use 'cause you had to carry everything yourself if you wanted it later.

We humped up and down mountains. Sometimes we'd stop for the night on mountains so steep you had to notch out a place in the ground for your butt, and then you had to jam your heels into the slope, and that's the way you had to sleep.

I did some idiot things in contact. I'd played war games when I was a little boy—you know, hide 'n' seek, cowboys and Indians (I was always an Indian.)—and I acted a little crazy, like a kid, when I was fighting. I thought I was brave.

I guess I was brave. So were others. We were doing right. But one guy, a city black, knew better. He told the lieutenant smooth out he'd had enough, he wasn't taking another step in the jungle. He threw down his rifle and got on a resupply chopper. The lieutenant was screaming at him to get out, and the black guy was screaming at us that we were the crazy ones. "You're all gonna die if you go in there!" he told us. He flew back to base camp, and we never heard from him again. I remember thinking he was a troublemaker and a coward, but soon I realized he was right. He was streetwise, he understood death and war; he'd seen it back home. I was just a little B.A. Indian boy who was playing at war, trying to be a hero. His were the words of wisdom.

Because I was an Indian, a lot of the guys thought I had some power. They wanted to be close to me in contact. I would protect them somehow. They used to say, "Whatever you do, stay with that Indian!" Everybody called me Chief, and they liked me to walk point because I was good at it. I could smell gooks. To me, they smelled just like pigs. I always knew when we were coming up on one of their camps. They are just like other humans: they eat in one place, sleep in another, and have their latrines someplace else. When I was a little boy, my grandpa kept hogs, and I always recognized that smell. Gook shit smelled like hogs to me.

The day I got hit, I was sure I was going to die. It was scary. I had respect for the NVA. When they shot, somebody was going to die. About nine in the morning we stopped for a water break. Way we did it, one guy from each squad would round up the canteens and go down to the stream and fill them. No big deal. But when these guys get to the stream, there are gooks down in the water playing grab-ass. Well, the shit started and it turned into a goddamn big deal. Contact lasted all day until after dark. Our CO was shot; the battalion commander came in snooping around to look in his chopper, and he was trapped and shot. Even Top, the first sergeant, was shot. When it was over, we had thirteen killed and fifty-one wounded.

We had stumbled into an NVA battalion. It was confusion. Squads were cut off from each other, guys got lost, our own artillery was landing on us, gooks were running through our perimeters. We crawled here and there. We crawled up to bring back our dead and wounded. The bravest thing I ever saw was this medic we had just got. He was a slob and a wimp, a fat guy. He was scared shitless; no excuse for him to be in the field. We had guys screaming for medics. Now a medic has one job, and that's to go up when someone's hurt, period. Guys were hurt and screaming, and this fat guy was laying there not moving. I got pissed and told him to get his ass up there and get those guys. Now he was scared, trembling, about to cry. Bullets were hitting all around us. The guy didn't want to go, but he did. He went up there and saved those guys. That took a lot of courage, that was brave. If I had done it, it wouldn't have been brave because I was about half-crazy. But this poor guy was scared to death and did it anyway. He got shot, but he was still brave.

My squad was going to circle up and go up a trail to bring back some more bodies. We ran into some B-40 fire right away. We lay down behind some trees and the RPGs exploded around us. There was this bright flash right in my face, and I thought it was my buddy firing over my head. I said, "Ted, quit that." But he said it wasn't him. Then it happened again: a bright flash right in my face. It was an RPG that went off right above me on the tree. The blast lifted me off the ground. I knew I was hit. I was burning like hell and bleeding all over. I did a two-second backward low-crawl out of there.

Our own artillery was landing in our perimeter. You could hear the puff of the guns as they fired from the hill and then the whistle as it went over us and then the crash of the explosion. But the crashes started getting closer until they were landing on top of us. I knew I was going to die. The lieutenant was screaming into the radio, "You're killing us!'' The rounds were cutting down the trees we were wrapped around. Guys were getting blown away. One guy took a piece of shrapnel the size of a shot put in his side. I remember going past being scared into being mad, really pissed off. I was only twenty years old, and there were all those things I hadn't got to do. It was one thing for the gooks to kill you, but your own artillery?

Black Cat Two-One

Bob Ford
Shawnee . . . Hue, 1967–68
Helicopter Pilot, 282nd Assault Squadron

Jerry McKinsey, Black Cat Two-Four, was a great pilot. Better than me, and I was Black Cat Two-One, section leader, and I wasn't afraid to fly into a hot LZ the size of a golf green day or night.

Jerry's ship and mine were on an ammo supply mission to the ARVN at Hung Hoa, three klicks from Khe Sanh. We tried to come in. We drew beaucoup heavy fire. The ARVN were surrounded. Their American adviser screamed at us over the radio not to come in, but any time we heard an American voice needing help, we came. Period. I told him on the radio, ''We'll come in again, and we'll kick the stuff out the doors.''

They didn't have much of a chance. Under siege for nineteen days, it was going to take a combat assault to save them. We loaded up five slicks and two Huey gunships. Stiner, McKinsey, and me. We flew these missions for the attaboys. We called them attaboys because when you flew missions for the ARVN, no one knew about it, or seemed to care, and a pat on the back was all you got.

Flying in again to Hung Hoa, we were hit hard. The place was overrun, and we sat our ships down right on top of the NVA. B-40s were going off all around, and we were taking small-arms fire. None of the sixty ARVN we set down on the combat assault survived that I know of. We lifted off just in time, and as we cleared the LZ, I looked back. McKinsey's ship took a B-40 hit. The ship was on fire, lying on its side. I watched McKinsey run, but then he went back to help the door gunner, who was already dead. I saw an NVA raise an AK and shoot McKinsey in the back of the head. My last sight of the LZ was of it being swarmed by the NVA. Gooks were in the trees. They crawled over McKinsey's ship like ants.

Days later the co-pilot and crew chief somehow showed up. In the confusion, they had gotten away and E&E'd. They confirmed McKinsey's death. Mac had nineteen days left before he got to go across the Big Pond—home.

Our standard line whenever we were sent on some difficult, almost impossible mission was, "We haven't picked up anybody in Laos all day. Why not?" Some Special Forces types were in deep trouble over the border. They weren't going to make it unless someone came for them. Of course we would. We took off our dog tags and left our billfolds and other papers back in the rear. We made sure our M-16s were cleaned; we would fight if shot down. No MIA or POW for us. I had decided that long ago.

By the time we got to the LZ the guys were in bad shape. They were totally surrounded, about to be overrun. I guess I was a little crazy: I didn't think they could hit me. I remember flying into their muzzle blasts. I thought we had the best squadron in all of Nam. Maybe we were gung ho, maybe motivated, but when Americans were on the ground and needed help, we were coming in.

We set down. These poor guys started running for the ships, carrying bodies. Of all the extractions we made, this was the absolute pinnacle. The LZ was about the size of a couple of cars. Those Rangers were really crazy; they acted like it was nothing but a ride over to the PX.

When we flew supply into Hue during Tet, I was commander of a seven-pilot section. During a three-day-and-night period flying in and out of there, every pilot was either wounded or killed. We were back and forth out of Danang for twenty days. We had no communication sometimes because of the weather. We had about a quarter-mile visibility; we were going a hundred knots, three feet off the ground at times. We took in ammo and supplies to marines and ARVN in pockets in and around the Citadel. We took hits every day. Nerves got pretty bad. On one flight I had a major with me and he lost it. He assumed the fetal position for thirty minutes and screamed over and over, "We're hit! We're hit! Can you get us outta here?" I turned his intercom off so the crew and I didn't have to hear him.

It was wild. Confusion. Destruction. We were taking fire from below us on a street. I looked down and saw a guy driving a U.S. jeep with the big star on the hood. I looked again, and I saw that the jeep was where the fire was coming from! An NVA had commandeered the jeep and was driving the streets shooting his AK-47 at helicopters.

Hero

Billy Walkabout
Tahlequah . . . Phu Bai, 1967–68
Ranger Team Leader, 101st Airborne Division

They say I'm a hero. You know, the Legend of Billy Walkabout and all that. I keep telling people it was more that I kept getting into positions where I couldn't run. Depending on what newspaper or TV station you listen to, I've got anywhere between fifty-six and seventy-three medals. Me, I don't know. I lose track. I know it's a lot of them.

Some of them I earned, some are bullshit medals. I got my first Purple Heart and Silver Star just fifteen days in-country. We were overrun at Chu Lai. I earned that Star. Another Silver Star I got, though, was bullshit. It was at the mouth of the A Shau Valley when I was still a grunt. The citation read, "For conspicuous gallantry while singlehandedly assaulting twelve enemy on a hill." Shit.

Fact is, my squad was pinned down by a bunch of gooks with an RPD on a hill. We couldn't move. I carried the 60. The lieutenant told me to lay down cover fire so the squad could assault on the flank. The thing was, though, I couldn't move. Where I was, they could look right down on me if I raised a hair. I was scared bad. I waited, listening for a pause that would mean they were reloading the RPD, then I jumped up and just ran a figure eight up the hill, firing a long burst and screaming.

I killed a lot of them, and the rest ran. This happened in just an instant ya gotta know, and it was crazy. I jumped in a deep hole at the same time as the one gook left on the hill jumped in the same hole. I landed on top of him and broke the stock of his rifle. I dropped the 60 outside the hole when I jumped. I was reaching for the .45 I carried and the gook hit me and broke my nose. It was crazy. The guy was trying to reload his rifle, and I was trying to get out the damn .45. We were both screaming for help.

I jumped out of the hole and tried to get away, and this crazy gook grabbed hold of my leg and pulled me back in. Y'know, like in a cartoon where the guy is hanging onto a cliff and slowly loses his grip? Y'know, he leaves his fingerprints in the dirt as he falls or gets dragged? That was me.

He was hanging onto my legs and banging my ribs, going crazy, and I was sinking back down in the hole. I was scared shitless. This mother's gonna kill me. Somehow I managed to reach my knife, and I just twisted around and stabbed him in the head.

When the lieutenant and the squad came up, I was still in the hole with my face bleeding, holding my ribs. The dead gook was at the bottom of the hole with my knife still stuck in his head. The lieutenant looked down in the hole and said, "Walkabout, that's the bravest thing I ever saw." Then he yelled at the men and pointed at the ground, "Look at that. The guy was trying to get away and Walkabout pulled him back in and killed him. I've never seen anything like it!"

People started flying in. All kinds of brass. And with each one of them the lieutenant took them and showed them the fingernails in the dirt. The general came in, and he shook his head and said, "Look at that." I tried to tell them they had it wrong, that the gook was killing me, but nobody was listening.

By the time I got to the Ranger company, it was sort of a bastard unit. They'd send us on tough missions. They hung us out to dry a lot, but we were good in the jungle. You know that movie where they make a big deal out of saying, "Terminate with extreme prejudice"? Hey, I had that said to me for real.

I saw some really bad shit, man. The worst was we found that cav team that was lost. When we found them, they were hanging upside down, skinned alive. I threw up. That really got to me. I had seen all that death. I saw five marine heads stuck on poles along Highway 1, I saw the mass graves at Hue. But none of that got to me like finding that cav team.

No one had to ask that question of me back in the States, "Did ya kill anybody?" Hell, everybody knew. It was in the papers and magazines. On television. The story was spread across the U.S. They knew I killed people. People on planes came up and talked to me. People from Germany and England had heard about me. Lose the war? I didn't lose shit. Every firefight, we won. We lost at a table in Paris. Personally, I'm glad I made Ho Chi Minh write beaucoup letters to mamasan. I caused a mayhem of water.

I volunteered to serve. I saw a lot. Men died. Friends died. I got hurt. It was shit. It was awesome. Yeah, I'd do it over.

Tropical Lightning Strikes

Wilbert Brown
Tulsa . . . Pleiku, 1966
Infantry Scout, Twenty-fifth Infantry Division

Intelligence told us an NVA colonel wanted to defect. We were to go in and bring him out. Our orders were to not fire our weapons, to use only knives if we came into contact. We were dropped into the jungle and force-marched until we reached the location the colonel was supposed to be. When we got there, he was there, all right, but so were several others. There were several other officers and two Chinese. We got the jump on them, so they dropped their weapons and surrendered, except for one Chinese. He started running through the jungle. Now you don't run in the jungle, it just isn't smart, but we had to catch him. Three of us chased him, two on his flank, me in the middle. As we gained on him, I saw him turn and prepare to fight. He did fight, but we took him prisoner after fighting hand to hand.

Darkness caught us, and we couldn't get out with our prisoners and the colonel that night. To keep our prisoners from calling out, we forced them to sleep with our rifle muzzles under their chins. When we returned, we learned we had been dropped into an enemy rest camp.

As a unit, we were sometimes sent out just to scare and confuse the VC, let them know we had been there and could return again. We left warnings that lightning had struck and the dragons had appeared.

To be a scout, you had to be either the best or the craziest. You walked ahead of the company fifty to a hundred meters, checking the area as you moved through the jungle looking for the enemy. Scouts worked in two-man teams; you got used to working with your partner. My partner was another brother, and we worked well together.

The company leadership considered me a morale problem because I had stood up to a white lieutenant when he was in the wrong. He was on my case, and I felt the leadership was out to get me. Later he apologized to me, admitted he was wrong, but the damage was done. They split my partner and me up. They gave me a white scout to work with. Our entire unit had gotten lost. We were looking for a bend in the river. We said go one way, the lieutenant said go another, and soon we were all lost.

The white scout and I were out front when I thought I saw something out of the corner of my eye. I told him to lay still and I'd go check it out. It was nothing, or anyway I didn't find anything. When I came back to the other scout, he was gone. I was scared. I thought the VC had him. I mean, in the jungle any distance is a long way to be separated from your unit. You are really out there on your own. I looked around for the other scout, but he wasn't anywhere in the area. Gone. I hurried back to the main unit. They were gone. They had left me. I was alone. I was lost!

The feeling. The feeling was terror. The jungle is hard to explain to anybody, even another Vietnam veteran. It is vast and terrible. What was I gonna do? I was afraid of being taken prisoner. That had always bothered me, and now it looked like that may be what was going to happen—if I didn't die first.

But for the grace of God I would have died in that jungle as alone as a child or been made a POW. As it turned out, I wandered aimlessly in the jungle for hours and hours until I came to the river. I was so alone and hopeless I just sat on the bank and skipped rocks over the water like when I was a little boy.

After a long time I heard movement in the brush behind me. I thought to myself, "Well, here you are. Are you gonna fight or let them take you?" The instant I saw the brush move I hit and rolled. This was the action my partner and I had worked out in training in Hawaii. If I saw the enemy, I would hit and roll and my partner would hit and roll the other way. This was also used if we got in front of each other. Like I said, we worked well together.

I was about to fire when I saw the point man hit and roll away from me. It was my old partner. We recognized each other. The sergeant was screaming, "Kill the mother!" but my buddy wasn't shooting. The unit was moving forward for battle. I kept rolling and the sergeant kept screaming, "Kill him!" Then my partner jumped between me and them.

I ran up and yelled, "Man, why did you leave me?" My buddy looked at me like I was a ghost and said, "We were told you went back to base camp." Bitterness is not the right word for what I felt. I was a troublemaker in the eyes of headquarters. They wanted me lost. They wanted to see me die in the jungle.

I was well trained in guerrilla warfare, and I became good at being a scout. But in war even the best can make mistakes. I was far in front of the unit, moving through the jungle, when I walked into a grove of trees. As soon as I was inside the trees, I sensed something was wrong, very wrong. "Damn," I said, and I looked around me. I was surrounded by people pointing rifles at me; I had walked into their ambush. I waited for the bullets to tear into my body. I was helpless. I let my rifle barrel droop. What was the use? I was a dead man.

To this day I don't know what really happened. Why did they let me go? Why didn't they take me prisoner? Kill me? One guy stepped forward and motioned at me with his rifle, and I figured he was going to be my executioner, but he said to me, "Same same, no fight," and then he and all the others melted into the jungle. Later that day, we made contact with them in another location.

I've wondered what he meant by what he said to me. Did he mean that since I was black I was the same as the Vietnamese, that I was a brother? Was it a single, isolated act of compassion, sparing my life? If they wanted to ambush my unit, which was obviously the idea, why didn't they just kill me with a knife or take me away as a prisoner? Why did they let me go? They had to know I would go to my unit and warn them. In my mind I still don't know why they let me live. Yet everybody carried guns, friend and foe. In a split second you had to determine who you were confronted by. If wrong, you paid the supreme price: death.

Prisoner Of War

David Price
Hominy . . . Saigon, 1967–68
Counterintelligence Scout, Military Assistance Command,
   Studies and Observation Group

I spent a lot of time on the other side of the DMZ. In the north, in Laos, Cambodia. You ever heard of lost-identity missions, where they take away your ID cards and anything associated with American citizenship, even down to clothes? That's what we went on. We had to wear civilian clothes or European-type uniforms, European boots and weapons.

I was so young, naïve I was like clay, moldable. They shaped me any way they wanted to use me. I learned languages. I felt professional, capable. I was gung ho. I wasn't afraid I wasn't coming back.

We would drop in with no radio contact and go do whatever Intelligence wanted us to do. It was mostly observation. We could call in artillery on most anything we found in Vietnam or Cambodia, but we were not to make contact if we could help it. Out there it was like being one lonely ant going across the street by himself. It was made clear to us that if we were ever separated, we were on our own, we didn't belong to anybody. We learned to divorce ourselves from emotion.

I was captured on an observation-type mission inside Cambodia. We were observing two regiments of NVA regulars. We somehow crossed their path. They found us in a riverbed. We were lying down, filling our canteens, when they walked right up on us. It's pretty hard for a few guys to run from a regiment. They shot four of us—just to keep us still, I guess. They tied us up, separated us, then got us back together. The four guys they hadn't shot, they skinned alive and made us watch.

The first six months, they tortured us constantly. They couldn't figure out just who we were. We all had on different kinds of clothes. I had the maps when we were caught, so they thought I was important, an officer maybe. I told them what we knew, which wasn't shit, but they didn't believe me. It bugged them.

It was sheer humiliation for eighteen months. They did whatever they wanted to with us. They constantly moved us through the jungle. When we were able to work, we did the most menial jobs. We worked the rice fields for them. They kept us isolated. No contact between Gary, Bruce, and me unless in work groups. The first six months, they kept me in a connex buried in the ground.

We were led into villages so the people could gawk at us. The NVA would say, "This is what you're fighting, so what are you afraid of?" I had malaria and amoebic dysentery. I lost from 185 pounds down to 125. I was the walking dead. In one village they tied one of our guys behind a water buffalo. You remember how those buffalo reacted toward white men? Their smell? The poor guy was dragged through a rice paddy.

It was hard time. They broke my hands. They tied my hands to a table and beat them with bamboo poles until they broke. The bamboo was split so every time they lifted them it would rip the skin. They broke my feet. They took an iron bar and hit me across the top of my feet. I learned to walk on the balls of my feet. The worst part, though, was when they tried to pull me apart. See these scars on my legs? They drove steel pins into my thighs and tied ropes to them and then pulled in opposite directions. I would scream and cry until I passed out. When I woke up, they would do it again.

Emotionally I kicked back and talked to God. I learned you never bargain with God, you just leave it up to Him. I maintained a certain amount of inner strength. I just tried to survive each day, one at a time. I thought a lot about my family. I'm sure they thought I was dead. The government told them I was missing in action.

After about six months they let up on me. I learned you could stand up to them. One day a guy came up to me and hit me over the head with a board. I was already a bloody pulp, and he hits me and splits my head open. I was bound at the wrists and ankles. It almost knocked me down. I staggered back. I was cross-eyed. I guess I didn't care anymore. I don't know. Kill me. I'd had it. I backed off, and I looked at this guy, and I said, "Do it again." This shook him up, I guess, 'cause he dropped the board. After that they quit messing with me, except occasionally to take us out and whip us in front of villagers.

They moved us near a village close to the border. Bruce, Gary, and me were working in a rice field and they were guarding us. It started raining like hell, and the guards ran over and got under the trees. All of a sudden we heard rifle fire, and it wasn't gooks. We started running. It was a bunch of regular grunts who had stumbled onto us. They liberated us. They had no idea we were in the area. It was emotional. I had never seen guys cry out of happiness before, but there was a lot of that.

For three months the government kept us isolated, all three of us, in a hospital. They wouldn't let us talk to anybody. I didn't even know if my folks had been told I was okay. I couldn't even have a doctor or a nurse in my room without there being a government man in the same room. I was still a prisoner.

The Edge Of the World

Les Weston
Tulsa . . . Quang Tri, 1969–70
Platoon Sergeant, Fifth Infantry Division

On the DMZ we were both bait and buffer. Our own brass hoped we would get hit hard so they could send in the 101st and have a major battle. And we served as a buffer between the NVA and the ARVN. We were supposed to be on joint operations with the South Vietnamese, but to tell the truth I never saw the ARVN in the field. They sat back at Dong Ha on bunker duty, enjoying American luxuries while we took the heat.

Nothing we could do would be a surprise to the NVA up on the DMZ. They were units of the 306th NVA and the 325th NVA who had fought at Khe Sanh. They were tough, first-line troops. They didn't run; they dug in, stood toe to toe, and fought you. Never less than a platoon-size element.

Another thing going against us: Americans had been in those hills so long, and the NVA had watched them just as long. Every hill was bracketed and cross-bracketed for mortars, every avenue of approach was diagrammed, every field of fire was well known. There was not a single hilltop that wasn't shot up. We didn't have to dig in at our NDPs; there were still holes and fighting positions left from three years earlier.

At night we stayed in the holes, waiting to be probed, mortared, overrun, or all three. Our positions were overrun twice by the NVA. The intense feeling among the troops was that we were put out in those vulnerable positions as bait. We were to lure them in.

I had an RTO for nine months. That's a very long time in combat. We were close. You couldn't help being when you relied on each other in combat. We worked well together. No matter how rough the contact, he was always nearby. Of course, we were a primary target, and an easy target. A platoon sergeant and his RTO with that funny box on his back with the antenna sticking up are not hard to pinpoint. We assaulted an NVA position, and I felt an RPG go past me. It hit my RTO's gunstock. You couldn't even recognize him after what that RPG did to him. I know they were aiming at me; it was meant for me. I had a tough time getting over that. Although we lost so many men, losing this guy was the very worst thing for me.

The actual DMZ was supposed to be just that: a neutral area, an area between the sides where neither side could go for any reason. Of course the NVA used it every way they could and the Americans went by the rules and didn't violate the area. Except once. I was in on that one violation of the DMZ, and I was never so scared in my life. We had hit an NVA platoon on our side of the DMZ, and when we assaulted their position, we started taking mortars. We knew the mortars were coming from our side of the river, inside the DMZ. I suppose it was a combination of things: being hit so hard and so often by mortars, frustration, anger. For whatever reason, the CO yelled, "We're going for those mortars!"

We went into the D and it was like an entirely different world. It was eerie, frightening. Very, very quiet. It felt like the edge of the world. As we pushed farther and farther into no-man's-land, we didn't know what the next step would bring. We were where no American combat units had been before. There was no way we could know what to expect, but it didn't take a lot of intelligence to figure it wasn't good. We found wide, smooth trails where the enemy moved freely and with a lot of equipment. Communication wires were strung alongside the trails. We found boxes of Chicom grenades just sitting by the trails. We found equipment lying around. All of us were scared. We were used to combat; we'd had a lot of that. But this was much different. This was scary. We expected to be completely overwhelmed any second. We were totally cut off in the enemy's stronghold, and we were alone.

We didn't find the mortars, we didn't have contact, we didn't even see a single NVA, but there was the terrifying feeling that all hell was going to hit us in there. The CO called in, and for a while it sounded like battalion was going to leave us in there overnight. Fortunately, they changed their minds. If not, I believe some American troops would have disobeyed a direct order.

Sua Sponte

Stan Beesley
Tecumseh . . . Phouc Vinh, 1970–71
Reconnaissance Scout, Seventy-fifth Infantry Rangers

It was like we were a humping, gun-toting melting pot in our company. We had lifers, draftees, shake 'n' bakes (NCO school graduates), snipers, Jungle Experts, Green Berets, stateside Rangers, in-country Rangers, a couple of West Pointers, Pathfinders, and ex-grunts. We had a couple of grandfathers, a seventeen-year-old who'd lied about his age to get in the army, beaucoup eighteen-year-olds, nervous husbands, and terrified fathers.

We had some superpatriots and an ex-draft dodger, a two-time deserter, a Ku Klux Klanner, two Black Panthers, a bunch of former hippies, and a lot of guys who'd turn hippie as soon as they got out of the army. We had Democrats, Nixon lovers, and Nixon haters.

We had all kinds of religion, and we all probably thought a lot about dying, each man in his own personal way about that most personal thing of all. We had Baptists, Catholics, a Zen Buddhist, a Black Muslim, several agnostics. One guy was an atheist. One guy we had thought Jimi Hendrix was the Son of God. We had altar boys and one preacher's son.

We had a grade-school teacher, a rodeo cowboy, a preacher, a farmer, a cement finisher, lots of construction workers, an insurance salesman, a mortician. Yeah, really. He was a mortician. The guy was very good in the jungle. He walked point in high-top black Converse basketball shoes. I got to know him because he would come by and talk to my hootchmate, Lozano, all night in Spanish. I asked Lozano once what they talked about, and he told me they talked about funerals.

We had a ton of college flunkouts. We had young alcoholics and lifer alcoholics. There were two guys with serious smack habits; they didn't last long. We had all kinds of people, except rich boys. No rich boys. No senators' sons. And not many officers. In fact, I saw only one officer in the field my whole tour. In our company, rank didn't mean much. We went by missions. You could be a Spec 4, but if you had twenty or thirty missions you could be team leader, and a first lieutenant, if he was new in-country, could carry your radio.

Yeah, we had all kinds. Except for not being represented by the upper class, my company was like all the other combat units in Vietnam; in other words, democratic, a cross-section. Talk about your tired, huddled masses. Just on my team alone we had a black from South Carolina, a sniper from Georgia, an Okie, a streetwise Philadelphian, a Chicano from L.A., and a baby-faced ex-grunt from Virginia. If it all sounds too pat, like a paperback novel, well, go tell it to Selective Service.

Nothing is all bad, and I guess that's the way it was in Vietnam, too. You talk to guys about Nam and if you talk long enough, you're liable to see as many smiles as tears. Part of it was the camaraderie, the commonality of experience. Some of it was the acceptance of military BS. Grin and bear it. Laugh to keep from crying.

It's funny—curious—how you can find pleasure in tough situations. How, when you are deprived of luxuries or even common necessities, you can still make do and even prosper if you've got the right frame of mind. Like that firebase in Cambodia. Even in Cambodia.

Our team operated out of what I bet was the tiniest base the U.S. ever set up in Southeast Asia. I mean it was like a large golf green in the middle of nowhere. It was such a forlorn post they didn't even make beer and soda runs to us. And you had to be damn forlorn for them not to get beer and soda to you anywhere!

It was just our team, three or four 105s, and a couple of infantry companies. That's all. I don't think the base even had a name. At night we lay out listening to all the big firebases around us being hit. Some were so close it was like watching a giant fireworks demonstration. We were nervous anyway, just being in Cambodia. We didn't know what to expect. It was a different war. You heard so many things. One five-man team lay beside a trail and counted 350 NVA regulars march past them within touching distance. Here the NVA were using tanks and trucks. We had been on one mission out of the base, and we hardly got out of hollering range when we were hit and had to be pulled out.

We spent a month on that dusty spot, pulling patrols, manning the bunkers, expecting every night to be overrun. We awoke every morning overjoyed to be alive. We passed the time throwing knives and trading with the Montagnards from a village nearby. I have difficulty in explaining to people how quietly satisfying those few weeks on that jungle base were to me, even though we didn't have much and were in a potentially bad situation. Maybe that's the reason why: simplicity.

When we returned to South Vietnam and resumed our normal missions, we were relieved. We figured out the reason we had never been attacked on that duck pond of a firebase, except for small probes, was that we were just too small to bother with.

We looked forward to the rides back to brigade main base from Xuan Loc; I called it joy on the deuce-'n'-a-half. Those were when I was with the Ranger company in the 199th. They weren't air mobile like the Cav—the chopper unit was in Xuan Loc—so we had to ride out and back for our missions on a truck.

Along Highway 1, after a chopper picked us out of the jungle at the end of a mission and dropped us at Xuan Loc, the company driver would pick us up. It took about an hour on the road, longer if the villages were crowded for market day or if there were accidents on the road, which happened a lot with all the Vietnamese traffic trying to dodge the military vehicles.

It was probably dangerous, but it didn't seem like it to us. We yelled—no, we screamed—at every child, babysan, mamasan, and papasan along the road. We tore open C rations and threw them to the children and the old people. They scrambled after the treats and fought over them and laughed. We called to every woman—from beautiful eighteen-year-olds to old black-mouthed shit burners—"Hey, Baby!" and we promised to marry each and every one of them.

Miller, our TL, had to remind us to watch the sides of the highway for ambushes. We were careless on those rides. We took off our shirts and drank beer. It was so good to be out of the jungle. It was good to not have to whisper. It was good to yell and look at the countryside and look at the people in the villages. You had to remind yourself that between the hootches or behind the French-built stone walls VC could be crouching with AKs and RPGs. It was fun. No other word for it. If someone had told me I would enjoy anything about Vietnam, I wouldn't have believed it. But it is the human way. Man is going to find some way to relax even in the worst of situations. You can't look for death around every corner (I had told myself I would try not to sleep for 365 days and that way I would stay alive in Vietnam) or you will wind yourself so tight you'll twist away.

Once we went through one of the quiet villages, slowing down for papasan and his buffalo, and we saw this beautiful girl in a saffron ao-dai. She carried a delicate parasol and leaned against a Shell sign. She was the most beautiful girl I had ever seen. She was a princess. Jimmy Knotts fell instantly in love. He took a John Wayne bar out of his rucksack, sidearmed it toward the girl, and yelled, "Here you go, Baby, be my girlfriend." The candy bar smacked against the sign, and the girl didn't act like she saw it. She looked at us and lifted her hand slowly and shot us the finger and said, "Fuck you, GI."

We had this drill sergeant in AIT, a little bitty Cajun. He'd been about three tours in Nam, wounded several times. A hard case. One time we were goosing around in the stands before a class on ambush tactics, you know, playing grab-ass and messing around trying to stay warm and beat the boredom. All of a sudden this little Cajun is right in the middle of us madder than a hornet, slapping guys, jumping from row to row knocking off steel pots, and throwing guys out of the stands. When he's done, he is red in the face and breathing hard. He rips open his starched fatigue shirt, and there is a scar down his stomach. He screamed at us:

"Listen up, girls. I been to this chickenshit little war y'all fixin' to go to and I survived because I'm a helluva soldier and 'cause me and Ho Chi Minh are some kinda distant kin. I snuck up to Hanoi I first got in-country and I told Uncle Ho I was damn sorry I was go'n have to kill beaucoup his boys, and he say, 'That's okay, just leave some babysan to fool around with.'

"They left me over there long enough, I woulda won the goddamn war my own self. But no, they say I gotta come back and train you sissies, teach you somethin' so you can come back home to mama with your little things still tucked between your legs. I tried, but it ain't no damn use, and I'll tell you why. 'Cause you, all of you, go'n die. And I'll tell you why. 'Cause you gotta fart 'n' giggle. That's right. You can't help it, but you just gotta goose 'n' grin. And, you'll die for it.

"Now the little man, he'll ball himself up in a little bitty ol' position you big fat-asses can't even get into and he'll stay like that for twelve hours and never twitch a muscle just on the off chance that he'll get one shot off at you! But you? Hah! GIs can't do that. They gotta fart 'n' giggle. Oh, you'll try. You'll try real hard—for about ten minutes. You'll set up on ambush, and you'll use all that good training we gave you, and you'll be real still and quiet— for about ten minutes. And then you'll get to thinking how nice it would be to have a smoke. And then you'll remember that candy bar in your pocket and you'll rustle around and get a bite. Then you might see a snake over there across the trail mindin' its own business, and you and your buddy you just got to mess with it so you throw a rock or two at it. Then pretty soon you don't see what it would hurt if you scooted over by your buddy so y'all could talk real low to pass the time. You tell a joke or two and lie to each other how your girl back home is being true to you and she ain't seeing Jody, and in no time the whole goddamn platoon is fartin' and gigglin' just like y'all been doin' here this mornin' and the little man is go'n sneak up on you and kill ever' swingin' Richard.''

Well, he got our attention with that, and of course we

believed him. He jumped out of the stands but before he left he told us: "Now, if any of you girls make it back, which I seriously doubt, come by, and I'll buy you a beer." Hesitating for effect, he paused in front of those cold bleachers and said: "I ain't had to buy too many beers these days."

When people ask me why I went to the Rangers, I tell them it was because of the caution factor. I was a grunt, headed for an infantry unit. I knew it was next to impossible for large units wearing steel pots and flak jackets to be quiet in the jungle. I figured my chances of surviving were better with just a few guys who were well trained and could move around in the jungle quietly.

As we were sitting around the pad at Long Binh—me waiting for the Ranger first sergeant in his jeep, the guys I'd come over with waiting for a Chinook to take them to the grunt unit on the border—we heard on the radio that Bravo Fourth of the Fifth was hit and lost fifty men. That was the company they were headed for. The one I had been assigned to before I volunteered for the Rangers. At that moment it seemed like a good choice. Even at that, though, my buddies tried to talk me out of joining the Rangers. "You're crazy, man," they said.

I was a draftee as far as the army was concerned, but I volunteered for the Ranger company. Only one time in my military career did I volunteer for anything.

You mention Ranger, people say back to you, "Gung ho." That's accurate. Or if not gung ho in the killer sense, at least most were well trained, motivated, conscientious, skilled.

A lot of grunts thought lurps (members of long-range reconnaissance patrols) were crazy for going out deep into the jungle in five- and six-man teams. We figured it the other way around. Our chances were better, we figured, because we could be stealthy. Or, like Lozano used to say, "we can outgook the gooks."

The first time we had a guy killed in our company in the Cav I had a hard time with the way it was treated. I was new to the company. I didn't know the guy. He was on another team. My team was on a mission, and we monitored the radio in the jungle and heard the report of him dying. We got back to the company area and they had a formation with the chaplain and the boots and helmet and bayonet and rifle. A short memorial. Everyone was torn up. Sad. Me too, and I didn't even know the guy. I went off to clean up, shower and shave, and my TL, Omer, said to me, "See you at the party." I said, "What party?" "Banta's party," Omer said. "I'll meet you at the club." This flipped me out. Here a guy dies, and we have a party.

Well, that night the whole company turns out for the biggest drunk you ever saw. All the free beer you could drink. There was a game you played called drink chuga-lug, drink chugalug. A guy had to kill a full beer while his buddies chanted this song, and if you weren't through with the can when they got through with the verse, you had to kill another one. Lots of guys came up short on purpose. It was quite a party. Guys laughed to keep from crying.

At first those memorial parties turned me off. Sarcastically, I said to Omer, "I get killed, you guys'll be so torn up about it you'll go get drunk. Some buddies." It wasn't right. But after we had had a few parties I began to understand. I don't expect anyone who wasn't there to understand and I wouldn't even try to explain it, but I came to realize that it was the fitting thing. For us. In Nam. I still felt that way even when Omer was killed.

Incoming

David Samples
Sapulpa . . . Dong Ha, 1966–67
Seabee, U.S. Navy Mobile Construction

I was nineteen years old. I was in the Seabees, and a
helicopter had dropped us the day before at a base known
only as A-3. It was located on the DMZ midway between
Gia Linh and Con Thien, reportedly the farthest north any
American troops had ever been. To say that the place was
pure hell would be a gross understatement. It was pure hell
to the tenth power.

Sixty of us had been sent there to build bunkers in
support of some marines I knew only as 1-3. The base was
completely surrounded by NVA and was being pounded
almost constantly by rockets, mortars, and artillery. Incoming. Every helicopter that came in drew fire, and the
one we were in was no exception. Welcome to the war.
Within a couple of hours of landing we were working on
our own bunker we would sleep in. About a dozen marine
engineers were stringing barbed wire on the perimeter
when a short barrage of mortar fire landed among them.
They were about a hundred meters from us, and I looked
up in time to see one of the poor bastards, or what was left
of him, crash back to the ground. A mortar had landed
between his legs. I had never see anything like that, but it
was not to be the last.

About four or five of the engineers had been hit and a couple killed. When the barrage ended and people were running out to help, we learned a painful lesson: the barrages came in pairs. When the second barrage hit, there were several dozen people there trying to help. From when the first barrage hit until the second one was over took less than three or four minutes, but the toll was many dead and wounded. The place looked like a human slaughterhouse. I staggered around, and my senses began to slip, and for some reason I cannot explain, I stopped to pick up a flak jacket on the ground. I jumped back when I saw what I had done. Most of the front of the jacket had been blown away, and it was saturated with blood. I ran back to work and tried to work away what I had seen. I was like a madman. I sawed timber and drove nails and ducked more incoming.

The rest of that day and that night was more of the same. Work, hard, back-breaking work. Hauling treated 12 × 12s by hand while being shot at and mortared. More and more men were killed and wounded. Helicopters brought in supplies and troops and took out the wounded, the spiritually shattered, and the dead, in that order of priority.

Inside our bunker we listened to the artillery war go on. There seemed to be never more than a few seconds' silence between incoming and outgoing. Sleep was almost impossible. The next day, somebody decided a bunker was needed near the LZ to provide cover for those coming and going troops. Eight of us were volunteered to build it. Being so close to the helicopter pad meant that every round aimed at a helicopter had a good chance of hitting us. The LZ was so close that the wind of the choppers was blowing down our 12 × 12s before we could nail them in place. But the work progressed; the helicopters landed and got shot at. We ducked and were scared. Some guys had begun to crack. One of our guys wouldn't leave the bunker. He begged us not to send him out there to die. The bunkers were much safer. A general was supposed to fly in that day and view the place, but an artillery round hit the command bunker and killed a major. One of his aides told me that the major had a cookie in his mouth when a large piece of shrapnel cut his head off. The general viewed the place from several thousand meters in the air.

A friend of mine and I were eating C rations while the helicopters landed and were shot at. Five times we had to stop eating because of incoming rounds. To this day I still eat too fast. But as we sat there eating and resting, something strange began to happen to me. I began to see my friend wounded badly—all in my head, of course, but the vision was very real. My friend, Huestis, and I had been working side by side for a day and a half, but now I became very uneasy around him. We started back to work and I was holding a 12 × 12 as Huestis nailed it down. The vision came to me again. Why, I will never know, but I walked the twenty-odd feet to the other end of the skeleton bunker and looked back at Huestis when a round hit between his feet. Everything took on a strange slowness. I saw the black smoke and red fire from the round. Huestis turned a lazy, slow spiral through the air and landed on his back. Another guy, Thompson, was hit too. He did a back flip to the edge of the hole we were in. I felt shrapnel whip the air around my head. The concussion then hit me and flattened me. I lay there in the worst fear I had ever felt in my life. Rounds kept hitting until the helicopters that drew them lifted off. There had been no warning whistle. The shell got there first.

I could hear Thompson crying for his mother and Huestis gurgling blood. I could hear and see others praying and crying. Crying for mother was the most common. Then and there I reached a decision. How much could I let fear control me and still live with myself later? I somehow managed to get up from the ground and run to Huestis' side. I was still crazy and mad with fear, but I knew that if I didn't make even a symbolic act of helping a friend I could not ever live with myself again.

It was sad. Huestis had his right arm almost completely severed, and his chest looked like Swiss cheese. His foul-weather gear had fallen over his eyes. I had seen his helmet fly past me. Blood and air bubbled out of his chest. I tried to stop the blood by sticking my fingers in the holes, but the holes were too many. I knew that the second barrage was on the way. Right on schedule it came. I covered Huestis' body with mine. Rounds hit. I was so scared. I wanted to crawl under Huestis instead of laying on top of him. But I couldn't do that to him or me. When the rounds let up, I screamed, "Corpsman up!" They came. One came up to Huestis, took one look at him, and pronounced him dead. I'm sure I could have been stabbed and it wouldn't have hurt any worse. My mind could not accept that, and I grabbed the corpsman and screamed at him. I remember him looking in my eyes, I guess checking to see if I was going to be all right. And then, to satisfy me, he checked Huestis again. He pulled back his flak jacket. Most of Huestis' chest was blown away; even his dog tags were gone. I dropped. As the medic moved to go to Thompson, Huestis kicked and moved. I grabbed the corpsman back, and he even got excited that maybe Huestis had a chance. He pulled Huestis' hood back to look in his eyes. The top of Huestis' head had been blown away. Everything past the eyes was gone. That was why the helmet had flown by me.

The medic checked me for wounds. I did not know if I had been hit or not. I went over to Thompson. Before I even got to him I could see he was going to die. He still called for his mother. It was very sad.

That night in the bunker we talked about Huestis and Thompson. When we loaded Huestis on the stretcher, his arm fell off, and I put it on the stretcher between his legs so it wouldn't roll off. Several people still held out hope for Thompson. I realized they hadn't seen how bad he was hit. They weren't aware as I was that he was going to die. I told them his wounds were too bad, he wouldn't make it. The mood turned uglier. The chief in charge came over to me and said that he wished I hadn't mentioned about Thompson. I was sorry I had. To make up for my stupidity, I started telling jokes. Bad jokes, old jokes, just anything to break the mood. It began to work. Slow at first and then faster. First one of us and then another would tell one, and pretty soon we were all screaming with laughter. It was an odd setting.

Later, in another part of Vietnam, I was going on R&R. I had once again allowed myself to think about the future. What would I do on R&R? I was excited. I wanted to buy a real nice stereo and send it home. I had a list of things my buddies wanted me to pick up for them. So very much to think about. It was a lazy, hot day, and I was standing in line waiting to get on the airplane. There we were all out there on the strip when the first round hit. It seemed like it took forever for it to soak in that we were being attacked. Panic tried to set in again. I shook inside. Others were going crazy. Then I remembered I could control my fear. It was hard, but I forced myself to calm down. No one was getting inside the bunker because of the panic. The door was jammed. More panic. We finally got the door open and got inside. Some never got over the panic.

New Pilot

Robert Kirk
Oklahoma City . . . Danang, 1969–70
F-4 Fighter Pilot, 480th Tactical Fighter Squadron

In our unit it was SOP (standard operating procedure) that if there were new pilots they would be teamed in the F-4's with veterans. Never two new guys together. It was an experienced man with a new guy.

A pilot just in-country was assigned to me. Our mission was to make a bombing run in a horseshoe valley, one way in, one way out. It was going to be a marginal mission anyway, but with a new pilot along the parameters of success were narrowed considerably. He seemed like a capable enough guy, had it together, but you just never knew how anyone was going to react in a tough situation until you saw him in one.

When we were near the target I quit worrying. Coming over the top there are just too many things to do, tasks to complete, to have much fear or concern for things you can't control. Fear usually didn't hit you until the mission was over. You saw it in the faces of the other pilots. You didn't have to ask what happened. If a mission went well, fine, nothing much was said about it; you went on to something else. But if something went bad, you could tell right away. It was then you had to work the fear out.

We began the run and the new guy said on the radio,

"We're gonna come in at 400 knots, okay?" We were almost over the target and I thought, "No way, that's too slow." Four hundred may be fine for training runs, where you had plenty of time to make slow, easy turns, but it didn't work that way in the real thing, especially in this closed-in little valley. Faster was safer. I took the throttle for more speed.

The new pilot took the throttle the other way. I took the throttle. He took it back again. I knew we weren't going over 400 knots. We dropped the bombs, and the new pilot was making an incredibly long and gentle turn to get away from the target. We weren't going to make it. I was frantic, but there wasn't much hope because we were heading for the sides of the valley. It was like slow motion to me. The walls were closing in on us. Then we stalled. We didn't have enough power. The new guy screamed, "We've got no fire! We're not going to make it!"

I knew he was right. Still—though it was hopeless, even more hopeless than my first mission, when I thought we would hit the limestone ridges—I reacted. I jerked the stick as hard as I could and braced myself spiritually for the impact. I recall the thought I had at that instant: "Was it all for this?"

There were heavy clouds in the valley, and as the aircraft entered them I knew the wall was the next thing we would hit. I strained at the stick, and we went farther and higher into the clouds. The plane roared, and then, incredibly, the most wonderful thing—we burst out into the sun!

I was shaken, and before I could control myself, I let the new guy have it. I told him how incompetent and stupid he was and a whole lot of other things I regretted saying soon after. I ate him out pretty good.

PART FOUR

Getting Home

Love, Son

Don Sloat
Coweta . . . Dong Duc, 1969–70
Infantryman, Americal Division

(Don Sloat was killed in action January 17, 1970, while on a patrol near the village of Dong Duc. He was one of eight men the small eastern Oklahoma town of Coweta lost during the war. He received two Bronze Star medals for valor. Following are letters he wrote to his mother while he was in the army and from Vietnam. They are published with the consent of Mrs. Evelyn Sloat.)

1969 Ft. Polk, La.

Dear Mom,

We arrived here last night. I'm stationed at South Polk. Last night during formation we were saluting while they played reveille. I was using my left hand. (You're supposed to use your right hand, Mom.) Boy did I get a good cussing for doing that. The drill sergeant comes into the barracks at night and throws lockers on the floor and jumps into people so it's pretty rough sometimes.

Love,
Son

June 18, 1969

Well I'm glad to hear that Bill and Debbie are getting married. Wish I could be there. Well, there isn't much to tell of what has been going on down here. About all we do is spend all of our time out in the pure swamps getting ready to go to Vietnam. Mark is going to Ft. Gordon, Kentucky. Both of us should be home on leave again about the same time. We'll probably go overseas together.

Love,
Son

June, '69 Camp

Dear Mom,
We're going out to live in the swamps all of next week so it should be a long week.

I'll be glad when it's over with. I'm coming home on leave in about eight weeks.

Love,
Son

Oct. 4, '69

Dear Mom,
I'll tell you a little more about Vietnam. Right now it's raining. I guess monsoon season. It's rained 4 days now and I suppose it will rain until March. So I'll probably look like a fish by the time I get home.

These people over here are the funniest looking people. The biggest one is not over 5½ feet tall and weighs about 120 pounds. So I probably look like a giant to them. [Sloat was six-foot-four and weighed 215 pounds.]

It's really pretty country. Mountains all over the place.

I've been swimming twice. I'm still not out in the field yet.

Love,
Son

Oct. 21, '69

Dear Mom,
Boy last night was a long night. We had operations set up about 50 meters from our location. We had to stay up all night on guard. So I'm rather tired now.

We hump miles and more each day with about 70 pounds of stuff on our backs, plus I carry an M60 machine gun, and it really gets heavy. It gets me down.

Time really does seem to fly over here. Once you reach your destination for the day all you really have to do is sit around. If you get a small cut it turns into jungle rot. It's real bad. I've got it all over my hands. They are so sore.

Love,
Son

Oct. 28, '69

Mom,
There is not really much to write about. My hands are so sore from cuts, it's hard to write. I keep them soaked in medicine all the time. But they still hurt a lot.

It would be nice to take a long hot bath and go out to eat some good food for a change. We went out on patrol a couple of days ago and found this stream. It was real cool and we went swimming in it. I've got a cold from it now. Just my luck. Tell everyone hello for me.

Love,
Son

Nov. 2, '69

Dear Mom,

We are still up in the mountains. We are going higher all the time. Right now we are a few miles from the ocean. You can see for miles. It is really nice country if it wasn't for the war.

Love,
Son

Nov. 5, '69

Mom,

We've got about 6 more days left of this operation before we go into bunker line. I'm really looking forward to it. A much needed rest. We've been up here in the mountains for about 17 or 18 days now and I'm really worn down.

It's still rainy over here and it does get cold. Right now it's raining and the wind is blowing.

Love,
Son

Nov., '69

Dear Mom,

Hi. Well I hope that this letter finds all of you doing just well. I'm just fine myself. A little tired and dirty, though. You know how I feel about cleanliness . . . well this is my 20th day without bathing. I've never felt so dirty before in my life. As soon as we get into bunker line I am going to fix that. I can't tell if I'm getting a tan or if it's dirt all over me. I only wish that I were there to spend Christmas with you all. But no sweat. I'll be there next year!

I've got a couple of things I'll be sending home when I can find something to mail them in. They are an ARVN flag and a VC lighter. I got them while we were searching a village.

Write soon.

Love,
Son

Nov. 30, '69

Mom,

I'm sending you some more film this time to develop. I think that all of them are of us out in the field. There is one in there with my pack on so you can see how heavy we hump. The pack weighs about 70 pounds and the gun about 30 pounds. So I've been walking and crawling around with about 100 pounds on my back ever since I've been here.

I think that we will get out of the field for Christmas because we've already been out here for 11 more days. I believe we've got about 24 more days to go on this operation. I believe the dinks are as afraid of us as we are of them.

Love,
Son

Dec. 10, '69

Dear Mom,

We are headed back in from the field now. We are supposed to stay about a klick away from our fire support base and train the P.F. soldiers.

The way our luck goes though they'll probably send us back out into the mountains again. I hate those mountains.

We got into some leeches up there the other day. Those things are as big as a house. I woke up about one in the morning and found one on my leg. They really scare me.

Well guess what. I've been put in for another medal. I guess they think that I am really gung-ho or something. They told me I did an outstanding job and they were putting me in for another one. If I keep it up maybe they'll let me out of the field.

I guess you probably know this by now but Mark Hatfield got his orders for Nam. I hate to see him come over. But I know he feels bad about the rest of us guys over here and him not being here. I'm glad in a way he's coming because it'll help me out knowing that he understands what is going on.

You said that you thought I was in only one part of South Vietnam. Well, we are but they have to move us to other places sometimes.

Love,
Son

Dec. 18, '69

Mom,

I'm back in the rear area right now. I've got a pretty bad cold. Plus my feet are swollen up. We had to stay in the rice paddies for 3 days and nights so I'm trying to dry up now.

Some guys came out last night and told me that I was going to get the Bronze Star medal.

Mom, you said that you could take it a lot easier if I was taking it ok. Well I don't know who told you I was taking it hard but this is not bothering me at all. So don't worry about it.

Love,
Son

Dec. 21, '69

Dear Mom,
  Well I'm back in the field again after a couple of days
of rest. We go into bunker line the 23rd then standdown.
So we've got a few days ahead of us that should be pretty
easy.
  I'll have 3 months in the 25th of this month. That only
leaves 9 months to go.
  Time passes pretty fast over here as much as I hate to
say this . . . time passes faster when we are out in the
field.

                                        Love,
                                        Son

Dec. 24, '69

Mom,
  We're in bunker line now and taking it pretty easy for a
change. After this we go into standdown for about 3 days
of real good rest.
  Well I guess old Mark is getting ready to come over
here.

                                        Love,
                                        Son

Dec. 25, '69

Dear Mom,
  I won the Bronze Star again. This is the second one. I
guess I'm pretty lucky to get this one. I took a couple of
rounds in my back pack.
  Jimmy Campbell got hit over here. I don't know

how bad. I think he's supposed to be sent back to the World.

Love,
Son

Dec. 29, '69

Dear Mom,

I'm doing just fine. We go in for standdown the 2nd of January. I will be able to get the field off my mind for a while. I am planning to take my R&R around June.

Love,
Son

Jan. 6, '70

Mom,

We are back in the field again. I guess you can tell by the dirt on this letter.

They have stepped up operations to about 35 days now. So we'll probably be out this time until February. I could sure use some more food.

Love,
Son

Jan. 10, '70

Dear Mom,

I'm in pretty fair shape, long and lean. They have been working us pretty hard lately. That's the reason I've not been able to write very often lately. It seems they think we are animals or something. It's bad enough we've got to be out in the field . . . and then having to run patrol 24 hours a day. I guess I probably sound a little harsh. But the lifers are getting me down. I'm probably going to have to take my R&R before I expected. So that I can get away from this for a while.

I've just about got 4 months in over here. That means 8 more to go. I met this guy from E Co. on standdown that I played football with at Northeastern A&M. I was really surprised to see him over here. I guess the Army has got about all the guys I ran around with over here.

I guess you'd better start sending me some more packages again. I can use some of everything. Don't forget that pipe and tobacco. Guess I'll close for now. Give my brothers and sisters my love.

Love,
Son

Jan. 14, '70

Dear Mom,

Well I hope this finds all doing ok. I just finished taking a bath down in the river. It sure does feel good to be clean for a change.

I'm being put in for a special R&R to Thailand for 7 days. I don't know if I got it yet. The reason I'm getting it is because of the medals I've won. There is a lot of talk going around that we may get pulled out about May and go home.

Well I guess my old buddy Mark is over here by now. I sure hope he does ok.

I got your package yesterday with the pecan pie and cigars. All the guys said to tell you it was real good and that they could eat some more of it. (Hint hint.)

From the way your letters sound you are getting a lot of snow. I bet the kids really love it.

Well Mom I guess I'll close for now. I'll write again real soon.

Love,
Son

(Sloat was killed three days after writing this letter.)

Feeling the Pain and the Hurt

Bill Poffenberger
Tulsa . . . Mekong Delta, 1970–71
PBR Repair Barge, U.S. Navy

I used to blame Vietnam for my problems, but I don't do that now. I can't. When I got back from Nam, I tried to kill myself. I took a gun, but it slipped out of my hands and blew a hole in the ceiling. Today, sometimes I just want to aim my bike at a semi. End it. I hurt a lot sometimes. I took drugs a lot in Nam. It was easy to get. I didn't want to feel the pain and the hurt. I lost a couple of good buddies and I just got strung out. If I die, well, at least I won't feel the pain. That's what I told myself. Two of my friends were hit by that round coming through the dining area, and they screamed, and I couldn't handle it. I'd seen death on TV, but in real life I couldn't accept it. I was eighteen years old, just turned nineteen.

At nighttime there were lights on the river. Usually when the enemy was going to hit us, everything got quiet and dark. I was on the bow, and it was dead dark. You couldn't see anything but black. I shot a flare and saw two gooks setting up a tube. I opened up and the shit started. I was put up for some medals, Bronze Star or Silver Star, which never came through.

When I was coming into Nam at Ton San Nhut Air Base, they were loading a plane with bodies, dead Americans. That freaked me out.

Today it's hard for me to think about Vietnam. The other day I tried to watch *The Deer Hunter* on TV, and I couldn't do it. It was tearing me up. There is still a lot of hate in me today for the United States people. We were over there doing what we were told to do, doing what we thought they wanted, and now they want to forget us. We make them feel uncomfortable. They call us monsters and baby killers. Well, fuck that. It wasn't our fault. We were just doing a job.

For a long time I was ashamed of being a Vietnam veteran, afraid of telling people I had been to Nam. Not any more, though. I have a flag on my bike and decals saying I served in Vietnam. The truckers honk their horns at me. I am proud.

Getting Home

Marguerite Giroux
Oklahoma City . . . Bien Hoa, 1965–66
Nurse, Third Surgical Hospital

Getting home from Vietnam was an experience in itself. There was an airline strike, and we were stranded on the West Coast. I spent my first night home at Travis Air Force Base in California. I finally managed to catch a hop on a Reserve plane. When we landed at the Reserve base, a truck came out and met the plane and piled the men and their luggage on back, drove them to the road, and from there they hitchhiked home.

I was the only female on board, so I had it luckier. A Special Forces officer's family met him there and gave me a lift to a hotel. From there I called my family to meet me the next day. It was late in the evening when I arrived at the hotel, and I was hungry so I went to the snack bar. I was excited about being back in the U.S.A., and I wanted to talk to someone, to share my thrill at being home. The waiter was cleaning the counter very thoroughly when I told him I had just gotten home from Vietnam. He said, "You did? We're closing. What do you want?" Suddenly, I was tired, and the thrill was gone.

Being with my family again made up for it. They understood; they had followed my experiences by close attention to the news on television. But talking to others was much more difficult. Even my boyfriend asked me not to talk about Vietnam. After all, he hadn't been there; what could we talk about?

I stayed in the army until 1977, and the memories of Vietnam followed me everywhere I was stationed. The sound of helicopters nearly drove me crazy in Germany. When I heard a helicopter at night, it meant someone was coming to the OR, and I couldn't sleep. What was it bringing? How bad was it? That sound will always cause a knot in my stomach.

I'm proud of being an army nurse, and I'm proud of the work we did in Vietnam. For me, Vietnam is and always will be as if it were yesterday.

Bandages

Gary LaBass
Bixby . . . Chu Lai, 1970–71
Infantryman, Americal Division

My wife said I wouldn't talk about it. Being in Nam. I have not talked about it.

Twice in fifteen years, it's gotten to me. Once, when I was really feeling sorry for myself, I thought about Nam and everything that happened, and I let it get to me enough that I broke down.

Then, about a year ago at school, I was walking down the hall while the kids were at their lockers and changing class. I wasn't thinking about anything in particular, and out of nowhere this smell came to me. So sudden and so real. I smelled it. I couldn't get away from it. It was the smell of the bandages and the way they wrapped them on you in the hospital. I could smell them. Strong the smell was, and I couldn't clear my head of it.

I tried to be real calm, but I walked as quickly as I could down the hall and up the stairs to my office. Carefully, I closed the door and made sure it was locked. Then I sat down at my desk, and I cried for thirty minutes.

Returned Warrior

Danny Bruner
Broken Arrow . . . Central Highlands, 1968–69
Infantryman, Fourth Infantry Division

When a guy got hurt, you did everything you could for him until the medevac came. You constantly talked to him, telling him he was going to be all right, even when you knew he wasn't. It was all you could do.

My friend Jim Iseman died with me by his side. He was shot in the chest and just quit breathing. There was a guy beside him, hit in the leg, not hurt bad at all. When he saw Jim die, he got all scared, and he just died of shock. Crazy. Here this guy had it made, he had the million-dollar wound, he was going home, and he up and dies.

Years later, Jim's parents came all the way from California to see me. Man, that shook me up pretty bad. They wanted to know some things about Jim's death. They wanted to know if he suffered. Were his glasses broken? It was hard, but I told them the truth about it.

Except for a few close friends who welcomed me home—like George Hunsucker, who put a sign out front of my house saying, "Welcome Home, Creek Sneak"—I can't say much about white folks. But Indian people treated me great when I got home from Vietnam. At powwows they would honor the Vietnam soldier. He became part of the Warrior Society. He had jeopardized his life to protect the tribe. "You saved us" was the feeling. Indians make it a point to show respect to warriors. They sang special songs for us, danced the Gourd Dance. A respected and honored spot was reserved for the returned warrior.

Sprayed and Betrayed

David Carter
Lexington . . . Cam Ranh Bay, 1967
Mechanic, 483rd CAM Squadron

I am Canadian born, an American citizen by choice. I chose to be a citizen. I chose to serve in the military. Why? Because I read the Constitution, and I love this country. I had lots of opportunities to run to Canada. Canada, at the time, was considered my home. I could have gone to Canada and been respected by my peers. I didn't have to go to Vietnam. But it was my turn, so I did.

I call myself a citizen-activist, and some of the things I

say may be called radical, but that's okay. We've got to care enough to speak up because the Vietnam War is not over. Veterans are dying today from the service they gave long ago. American chemical companies and Veterans Administration denial of toxic poisoning will kill more veterans than did the Viet Cong. The Vietnam veteran has been sacrificed to protect corporate greed.

When I first came home from Nam, I was tied into the American dream and was naïve as to the true impact military service has on a citizen. I had a wonderful wife, who has been and still is extremely supportive, and within two years we had the first of two daughters and were building what eventually became a good business (gone now). I had symptoms, denied by the VA: malaria-like shakes, forgetfulness, grogginess, aches, angina, dizziness. But these episodes were like six months apart when they started. Therefore, any physical impairment was minimal. Everything was super until the symptoms increased in severity and frequency and became debilitating.

For a long time the Vietnam experience was not a good experience for me. But now, by expanding myself and my work through efforts to help the Vietnam veteran, I find my life to be a more positive experience.

Today, as a result of being exposed to toxic chemicals by my own government while serving in Vietnam, I am totally physically disabled. I have five chlorinated pesticides stored in my body. I suffer mixed-connective-tissue disease; my system produces antibodies to my own DNA; I have liver dysfunction; my immune system is damaged; and I have degenerative arthritis of the spine. Finding all this out meant a lengthy, frustrating, painful, and expensive medical and legal battle. The VA did not foot the bill, I did. My wife did. My family did. I couldn't get help from the VA. I worked with my family and other veterans to find those medical people and legislators who would listen to us, who would take us seriously. At one bitter point in this bitter struggle, I said, "This is a hell of a way for a veteran to find out what's wrong with him!"

About three years ago, I did a talk show on an Oklahoma City radio station and a fellow called in. He gave me my commander's name, my squadron's name, and he talked about my unit. And I said, "Were you stationed with me?" He said, "No, you were on our spraying schedule. We sprayed you every Thursday morning at eight o'clock." Our shops were right along the flight line. They sprayed our runway. We were on the spraying schedule. He had us nailed.

I had two friends, Vietnam veterans, kill themselves in the last year. We're seeing more and more vets ending up this way. Why? Are these veterans killing themselves because of what happened to them in Vietnam? We have all heard about the mental problems: the psychos, the druggies (Just a little sidelight here: folks say Vietnam veterans are druggies. The drug culture didn't go to Vietnam. They stayed at home.), the flashbacks, the posttraumatic stress, guilt, narcissistic injury. But there is something else. How many of these tragic problems have been chemically induced by toxic spraying in Vietnam? If someone in authority would really look closely at these deaths, it would be frightening. Some think the government knew that the things they were spraying to take away the enemy's hiding places could kill us. They knew it, and they did it anyway. Veterans need to be aware. They need to know that their physical problems are real, to give them credibility so they will quit killing themselves.

We know the things Agent Orange and the other toxic chemicals sprayed in Vietnam cause: cancer, birth defects, cardiovascular problems, liver dysfunction, and so forth, but what is really frightening is it has a lag time between exposure and disease manifestation. So if a vet were exposed ten, fifteen years ago, he may only now be getting ill from it. The lag time is now! This is when the vets and their children are going to start getting ill.

The General Accounting Office conducted a congressionally ordered study, and it was found that the government used so much Agent Orange, not counting the other toxins, that the U.S. Congress said in November, 1981, that every Vietnam vet must be assumed to have been exposed. They were dumping full planeloads at ten thousand feet. They dumped ninety-one emergency dumps, forty-one over U.S. bases.

What can a Vietnam veteran who has been damaged by exposure do? It's against the law for a veteran to sue the VA. If he does go through the VA appeals system, he can pay an attorney only ten bucks—just upheld by the Supreme Court yesterday. The Veterans Administration does not give the veteran the benefit of the doubt as required by the Uniform Code of Military Justice. U.S. Code 38. Well, the veteran can go through the civilian courts, so that's what we did with this suit against Dow Chemical. We hired an attorney who built an excellent case of discovery, sent it to a federal judge. The judge said a lot of evidence here says that the chemical companies knew how dangerous the stuff was and withheld information, so go ahead and sue. As soon as we had permission to sue, the Reagan administration immediately gave the judge a promotion. Our case went to another judge who said it was of doubtful merit. This judge immediately appointed a management committee of nine attorneys, who took a vote and fired our attorney. Now we're in front of a judge who doesn't like us, represented by attorneys we didn't hire! Then the judge takes ten representative plaintiffs (one is a good friend of mine), puts them in a hotel room in New York in an all-night session, and tells these fathers of crippled children and these sufferers of chronic severe pain that if they didn't take an out-of-court settlement—there's only going to be 17,000 good cases, anyway, and 17,000 into $180,000,000 makes it look like a big settlement—he would invoke contractor's defense, which means the contractors only did what the government told them to do, and the veterans wouldn't have anyone to sue anyway because the contractors will hide under sovereign immunity! Hence our "out-of-court settlement." It was jammed down our throats with no alternative.

If you read the Declaration of Independence, one of the main causes of the American Revolution was sovereign interference with the judiciary. That's exactly what happened to our case, and they're gonna get away with it. This isn't just someone trying to murder the Vietnam vet, this is messing with all Americans' basic rights. The apathy of the American public is going to let them do it. I have been told that the Reagan administration proposed that judicial review be removed from the Social Security System, citing the veterans' loss of judicial review as precedent.

I have become politically aware that the U.S. Constitution does not apply to the American veteran. I swore to uphold the Constitution twice: once when I became a citizen, once when I went into the U.S. Air Force. It is a wonderful document, the Constitution, and it should apply to every citizen, including Vietnam veterans.

Tricked

Danny Cruz
Tulsa . . . Phu Bai, 1967
Machine Gun Squad Leader, Twenty-sixth Marines

I see a lot of Vietnam veterans these days in my job, and I see something in their eyes that disturbs me. They all seem to have one thing in common: rejection is written all over them.

Despite my intense loyalty to my country, my strong feelings in favor of support of country, I can't help but think sometimes that the war was all a big trick. We were tricked. There are times that I dream of combat situations, and I think of those we lost, the waste of lives.

Immorality. I guess immorality is the right word, though a harsh word, for the war and everything that the war came to mean.

I feel this attitude most often when I am talking with a vet, especially when I am working with a vet having troubles. When I see the rejection in his eyes. It is then that I realize that what happened in Vietnam was not good for this country.

Learning To Love Again

David Price
Hominy . . . Saigon, 1967–68
Counterintelligence Scout, Military Assistance Command,
  Studies and Observation Group

It took a long time for me to come to terms with being an ex-POW. There was the stigma of being a Vietnam vet, and on top of that I was an ex-POW. I couldn't relate even to my friends. I was bitter and full of hate for the cruelty, for the extremes man could go to to hurt other people. I went through two wives. My wife now I was married to three years before she ever knew I was a POW.

I had trouble getting the government to recognize me. I went back to Nam two more tours because I felt I could do some good, I could help. I waived everything by going back. They made me sign waivers never to admit anything about what had happened to me.

When I left the army I was like a newborn baby. I did everything ninety miles an hour going nowhere. I wanted to do something. I had this empty feeling. There were hard times.

I was bitter about what the Vietnamese had done to me, what they had done to me physically and mentally, emotionally. By now a lot of Vietnamese had come over to America, to Oklahoma. You'd see them in stores. I would tell my wife, ''I smell gooks,'' and she'd say, ''Oh, c'mon,

Dave, don't be silly.'' Sure enough, a couple of aisles over we'd run into one.

Then a guy helped me, and it was in a way you would have never thought possible. I was drawn to this small church. I'm Catholic, and I wanted to start going to mass again. I went into this church. I walked in, and I looked down the aisle and saw the priest. He was Vietnamese. Here in Hominy, Oklahoma, was this little bitty Vietnamese priest.

He was a wonderful man. We hit it right off. We became very good friends, very close. He helped me in so many ways. He taught me to love again.

His name is Father Minh, and you know what? We have the very same birthday, November 11, Veterans' Day. How 'bout that? Father Minh is in Rome now. He sent me a picture of him and the Pope. Father Minh wants to get to Washington, D.C. He wants to go see the Wall. He wants me to meet him there. I hope I can. Wouldn't that be something, me and him at the Wall?

A Vietnam Love Story

Lee and Betsy Keyes
Tulsa . . . I Corps, 1969
Corpsman, Third Marine Division

LEE: There were two jobs open in my Reserve unit: clerk-typist and corpsman. I knew corpsman meant Vietnam because I was in the 2 × 4 program (two years of active duty with four years of reserve duty). The guy shot straight with me; he said corpsman probably means you'll go to Vietnam. He said go home and think about it before I signed the papers. I did. I went home and thought about it, then came back and signed the papers to be a corpsman.

I felt I could do some good in Vietnam. I wanted to help. For eight months in the States I worked with wounded marines who'd come back from Vietnam. I was prepared to go.

BETSY: My girlfriend's husband was in Vietnam. I was a sophomore in college. She told me a buddy of her husband's had just gotten a Dear John letter in Vietnam and she wanted to know if I would be interested in writing to this guy. I started writing in September.

LEE: Mail was important in the bush. I enjoyed and looked forward to Betsy's letters. I didn't get much mail from home.

*   *   *

BETSY: My father raised me to be a good devil's advocate. I could take either side of the war and the protest movement. There was the patriotic part of me and also the part of me that said everybody has the right to his opinion. And this is something that Lee and I have cussed and discussed many times, but for all the protesting that was going on, if it could bring the men home, that was all right by me.

LEE: Though a corpsman, I was basically a grunt. I didn't question when they handed me a .45. And when a guy would be dusted off, I would hang on to his M-16 until he rejoined the unit or I would send it in with the next guy out. It was fine and dandy to me. Geneva Convention rules didn't mean shit in Vietnam. I carried a little card with a red cross stamped on it that said the gooks weren't supposed to shoot me. Was I supposed to hold this up in a firefight and say, "Hey, here's my card, don't shoot"? Bullshit.

As I said, mail was important, but when we were on patrol I rarely thought of anything else. If you didn't pay attention, you were dead. However, Betsy's letters were a source of strength by giving me a feeling that I had her support.

BETSY: We wrote back and forth. We had to work around the lies in the letters. Y'know, we both wrote each other bullshit. Lee sent me pictures. In each one, he had on a hat. I wrote back and asked him, "What is it? Are you bald or something?"

LEE: Well, I am getting thin now, on top mostly. But back then I had more hair.

* * *

BETSY: I had polio when I was two, but I didn't dare tell Lee until it was absolutely for certain I was going to meet him face to face for fear he'd quit writing. I met Lee on June 1. We were married in October. Our entire courtship was by mail. Curiously, even today, written communication between us is the best way to talk to each other.

LEE: At first my only thoughts were of getting back to the World. I had a lot going on in my mind, but after a few days my thoughts came back to Betsy. I was very anxious to meet her face to face. It was like a child waiting for Christmas morning.

BETSY: If it hadn't been for Vietnam, Lee and I would not be together. Some good has come from it.

LEE: And also three children at home.

Despite those things that have worked out, I felt cheated in Vietnam in the sense that I didn't get to do more, help more. I was patriotic. By signing up to be corpsman, in effect I volunteered to go to Vietnam. I saved two men's lives, but I wanted to do more.

Gun Hill

Stephen Redman
Kellyville . . . Pleiku, 1966
Infantryman, Twenty-fifth Infantry Division

The night I was supposed to come home, there was this ARVN unit out in the field and they got hit. They called for support from Gun Hill. That's what we called it. Gun Hill. That's where the big guns were.

We don't know what happened. We never did find out. Maybe the ARVN gave them the wrong location. Our own guns hit one of our barracks. Guys never knew what hit 'em. Never even got out of bed.

A few years back, I was in the VA hospital in Temple, Texas, and a man came to me and said, ''I heard you were in Vietnam.'' He was the commander of Gun Hill. He's a nurse now.

I don't know if it's because of what happened that day. I heard back then he was real upset and he quit the army and said he was through with all of it. He didn't want no more to do with it.

The Deer Hunter

J.D. Maples
Muskogee . . . Firebase Bear Cat, 1969–70
Machinegunner, Twenty-fifth Infantry Division

Some friends said, "Let's go deer hunting." I'd been back from Nam and in college not too long, and I didn't think anything about it. We went out near Tahlequah. I got up in a tree with an old M-1 rifle. It was a beautiful day. I'm not in that tree thirty minutes when this beautiful buck strolls right into the clearing below me. I raise the old rifle, take aim, and put a round right between his eyes. I'm down out of that tree, slit the deer's throat, and start gutting him before my buddies can get over to me.

I'm down in the belly of the deer working away when my friends come up. I looked up and this smell came to me: a strong smell of gunpowder and blood. That combination got to me. I can smell it now. I got physically sick. I know it flipped my friends out.

We took that venison home and prepared it. I have loved deer meat all my life, but I couldn't eat it. I tried to, but I got sick again.

That should have told me something, but I didn't learn my lesson. The next year I went out hunting again with a different friend. I got settled up in a tree and wasn't there long when through the brush I saw a deer's head peeking through. All right! I raised my rifle and sighted right between the deer's eyes. I was ready to squeeze the trigger when the deer's head turned into a man's head! I put down my rifle and I was shaking, sweating. I'd almost killed a man. I looked up, and I saw the figure closer this time, and it was a deer. I stared very hard to make certain my eyes weren't playing tricks on me. I aimed the rifle and was about to shoot when the deer turned back into a man. I threw the rifle down. I was afraid to look again.

I was shaking. My friend came running up. "What's wrong with you?" he said. "Didn't you see that buck?"

I was still shaking, and I told him, "You say it was a deer. I don't know what it was. I wasn't going to take any chances."

That was fourteen, fifteen years ago. I haven't been deer hunting since.

Burying the Past,
Burying the Truth?

Kathryn Fanning for Hugh Fanning
Oklahoma City . . . Danang, 1967
Marine Fighter Pilot

For seventeen years I didn't receive any information about Hugh, though he was presumed dead in 1976. I could no longer remember the sound of his voice. I could remember only a few things he'd said. But I didn't have to close my eyes to picture his blue eyes, his lopsided smile.

During Operation Homecoming in 1973, I held out hope that Hugh would be among the returning even though I had no information which would give me hope. That day the marines called and said they would like to send someone out to be with me. I said, "Have you heard anything new?" They told me no they hadn't but that that in itself was not conclusive.

I watched each man appear in the door of the aircraft and walk proudly down the ramp. I prayed silently that Hugh would appear. I wept. But even before the last man appeared something came over me that let me know that Hugh would not be on that aircraft. I will not say what that feeling was . . . but it touched me with a powerful certainty.

When I was told that his remains were handed over by the North Vietnamese on July 17, 1984, the old pain balled up again, threatening to overtake me. I was shocked to find myself catapulted back into the past, back into those dark days, those days when I couldn't get the copper taste of death out of my mouth.

Dead! The original four-letter word. Hugh's funeral was a nightmare. Television cameras. Newspaper reporters crowded for a shot of the casket, and, again, the sense of living a horror movie came back. I didn't mind the media attention, in a strange way, because I thought that Hugh was due some sort of honor after his death in such an unpopular war.

The most painful thing . . . I resented never having the chance to be alone with his casket. Two marines in dress blues stood at attention at all times. When I asked if I could see the remains, I was told that it would be too upsetting. Later I learned why.

The following year, in July, 1985, I asked to see Hugh's file while I was in the Washington, D.C., area for a meeting of the National League of Families. Several times I had asked to see Hugh's official forensic report, hoping to find some mention of how he'd died. Was he killed on impact? Was he taken captive and tortured to death? If I couldn't have Hugh, at least I could have the facts.

Hugh's file revealed two sheets that sent chills through me. On one, reports told about his being identified as a prisoner of war by a North Vietnamese rallier in 1971. The navy concluded that the reports fit a navy returnee more than they fit Hugh. Some of the reports fit Hugh exactly, however, except for a single detail.

Regardless of the truth of the reports, why wasn't I told about them? I was upset. I asked the casualty officers,

Major Stew Cameron and Captain Art Gorman, why no one had ever mentioned the reports. Why not in 1971, when they were taken? Why not in 1976, when Hugh was presumed dead? Why not in 1984, when I buried what I was told were his remains? They couldn't answer. It was "before their time." I reminded them that I was always told that I would have any bits of information about Hugh, however small. These reports were hardly small!

I continued to look through the microfiche sheets in Hugh's file. In the back of the file there were several sheets of paper. On one someone had scribbled, "Prepare to receive the following remains: Right arm and 5 right finger bones. Partial right scapula. Partial right hip bone. Partial right fibula. Left tibia. Left fibula. Left one-half foot and ankle."

Suddenly, I couldn't breathe! Was this what I buried? A handful of bones? It had to be a mistake. When my casualty assistance officer, Major Richard Harmon, had called to tell me that the identification was positive, I asked him if the dental records matched the teeth. He told me they did. Maybe he had been mistaken, but no.

I later asked him to telephone the Central Identification Laboratory to find out if there was a bullet hole in Hugh's skull, since I'd had a vivid dream in which Hugh told me, "I have a hole in my head."

I remembered my notation in my journal. Harmon had telephoned me back, saying, "No. There's no hole in the skull."

Why didn't he tell me THERE WAS NO SKULL?

I called Captain Gorman over and asked him why I'd never received my forensic report. He said that he'd check. Later he told me that it had been sent to me last spring.

"Will you call Major Harmon and find out what happened to it?" I asked him. I flipped open my address book with Harmon's new telephone number at Camp Pendleton. "Maybe it got lost in his office when he moved and no one knows what it was. Maybe it's still at Tinker Air Force Base."

Major Harmon admitted that he'd chatted with his wife, Susie, and decided the report would upset me too much. I couldn't believe my ears. Since when did a marine officer discuss official documents with his wife and decide to remove them to his home on the basis of their chat?

It was obvious why he thought I'd be upset. I would realize that he had withheld the information that positive identification of my husband's remains was NOT made on the basis of teeth and skull as I'd imagined. I have difficulty believing that Major Harmon would make such a decision on his own.

After speaking with Harmon, I told Captain Gorman that I was going to make a copy of the positive-identification reports, as I got my tape recorder from my hotel room. When I returned to the temporary Casualty Office Gorman and Cameron were staffing at the Radisson Mark Plaza Hotel, I was unable to find the reports in the stack of microfiche. I examined each, one after another, fitting each into the viewer and patiently searching each line. I asked Captain Gorman to help. He also put each piece of microfiche through the viewer. No success. Had someone removed it in order to prevent me from making a copy? Perhaps.

The next day, I returned to the Casualty Office and helped myself to Hugh's file. There, the very first sheet on the stack, was the microfiche with the reports. How could I possibly have overlooked it? Or was it not there to be overlooked?

I slowly read each line into my recorder and put the file

back in place. The first thing I did when I got home was transcribe the reports and make multiple copies.

Major Cameron telephoned and told me that it had been recommended on July 22, 1971, that Hugh's status be changed from missing in action to prisoner of war on the basis of the reports. Obviously, the recommendation wasn't followed.

In a later telephone call, Major Cameron told me that he had gone through Hugh's file and couldn't find the microfiche.

"Don't worry," I told him. "I copied it. Would you like to have a copy of my transcript?"

He gave me his address in Washington D.C., but when I learned that he was coming to Oklahoma City on Labor Day, I decided to give it to him in person.

On September 16, 1985, I participated in a press conference in New York City with Green Berets Mark Smith and Melvin McIntire, who had filed suit against the government for suppression of information about live POWs; Jerry Dennis, who had proved that the purported remains of his brother Mark weren't accurately identified; and Anne Hart, who was given seven bone fragments supposedly her husband's.

After the press conference, in which I gave out copies of the POW identification reports from my husband's file, I received a telephone call from writer Jay Finegan with *Army Times*. Finegan told me that Captain Art Gorman of the Casualty Office told him that Hugh's POW ID reports didn't exist, that he had gone through Hugh's files a number of times and had never seen them.

"But he can't say that!" I protested. "They have the original microfiche, and they have a copy of my transcription. Major Cameron acknowledged them over the telephone later, too. Ask Major Cameron."

"He's on leave," Finegan told me.

Convenient, I thought. Major Cameron would be unable to lie about the existence of the reports, since we had discussed them and he had my copy. But Gorman? He could safely say he hadn't SEEN the reports. Were the marines trying to discredit me or was it simply a mistake?

I was puzzled. I telephoned Captain Gorman immediately. Why would he make a statement to a reporter in the first place, since that was the function of Public Affairs?

"You know those reports exist," I told Gorman. I quoted what Finegan told me.

"I'll have to stand by what I said, Mrs. Fanning," he answered.

I struggled to maintain some composure. "Look," I said. "Harmon already has mud on his boots regarding this case. Why do you want to make yourself look bad? You have the reports, I have the reports. How can you tell Finegan they don't exist?"

Gorman claimed that my transcript wasn't in Hugh's file, nor was the microfiche. He refused to contact Cameron for another quote on the matter.

For the first time, I suspected there might be a cover-up involved in Hugh's disappearance. Or was it all coincidence? Why wasn't the forensic report given to me BEFORE I buried the thirty pieces of bone? Why did Major Harmon encourage me to believe identification was made on the basis of dental material? Why had he removed my requested forensic report to his home? Why had no one alerted me about the 1971 POW identification reports? Why did Captain Gorman tell the *Army Times* that the reports didn't exist when he knew better? After all, I'd discussed it with him over a hamburger after I'd first read them.

COVER-UP. That nasty word was beginning to seem likely. There was no question in my mind that the Central

Identification Laboratory was signing questionable reports. The reports of my certified anthropologists, as well as those concerning cases involving several other families, made that clear. If the remains issues were being dealt with in such a questionable fashion, how were the 751 live-sighting reports of POWs being handled? I wondered.

I telephoned Mark Waple, the Green Berets' lawyer in North Carolina, and told him that I would sign an affidavit concerning the mishandling of Hugh's case. Later I was signed as a plaintiff in the case along with Smith, McIntire, Dennis, Hart, and Marian Shelton, the wife of the only officially listed MIA.

I am disheartened to discover that I was much more faithful to the Marine Corps than it was to me. I'd always believed the slogan "The Marines Take Care of Their Own."

My children, too, have been hurt by their new perception of the Marine Corps. My daughter Erin had decorated her bedroom with Marine Corps posters, had placed Hugh's medals and cover on her bureau, and had placed the now-dry floral arrangement that the marines sent to the funeral in a place of honor. Her mementos are still there, but her feelings have changed.

Now when I see a marine in uniform, the sadness and pride are tinged with bitterness. When I look at our bumper sticker, "The Few. The Proud. The Marines," I silently add, "The Forgotten."

Where is Hugh Fanning? Will I ever know the truth? Will those charged with the investigation of live-sighting reports reverse their tradition of stating that we have no proof of POWs in Southeast Asia? Or do they value their careers, put in jeopardy by their do-nothing pattern, more than their fellow Americans who risked everything in an unpopular war? Only time will tell.

I've been told that I'm wasting my time fighting the government. I've been told that I'm crazy for not burying the past. I've also been supported by hundreds of others who, like me, want the truth if nothing else is available.

Wherever Hugh is, he is not forgotten. I love him as much today as I did in those golden days at the University of Dallas. I see him often: in our daughter Erin's kitty-cat eyes, in our son Michael's offhand humor, and in our daughter Kelly's ramrod posture.

But I miss him and will never rest until I've done everything I can to find him. Dead. Or alive. If he was the one *you* loved, wouldn't you do the same?

Carrying George

Jim Howarth
Holdenville . . . Tay Ninh, 1968–69
Infantryman, Twenty-fifth Infantry Division

George and I were pretty close. George was the RTO for our platoon leader, who at that time was an E-5. We had more E-5s as platoon leaders than we did lieutenants. Lieutenants kept getting killed.

We were on a night ambush. Next day we were to go in and have a kind of day of rest, but we got orders to patrol the area instead. A thick area. Bamboo. Vacated hootches. We all walked single file by this one section, and we heard gunfire. The guy was in a spider hole. He took out the last two: RTO and platoon leader. Wounded the E-5 in the hand and hit George right in the heart. We killed the sniper, and to this day I think he was Chinese. He was taller and heavier. He was killed several times over because George was well liked by everyone.

I carried George's body to the chopper, and I was crying. I laid his body up in the helicopter. The E-5 was on a stretcher; his hand was bleeding, and he looked at me and I shook my head. Grunts. You could look a grunt in the eyes and know exactly what he meant. I knew what the E-5 wanted; he wanted to know, "Did George make it?" I shook my head and the E-5 just dropped. George had been his RTO. You get close. I always wondered about that E-5 riding back in that chopper with George's body.

After I came back home, George was on my head a lot. Today, George represents for me all those guys I knew but whose names I can't remember.

One day on the job, not this job, but another one—it was around Memorial Day—I could not get George off my mind. He kept popping into my mind. Me carrying his body. I tried to do other things, think about something else, but he kept coming back. I went home. I just left work without telling anyone. I could have lost my job. I had to find out where he was from. I had to find out who his parents were. I was possessed. It was something I had to do.

I knew he was from North Dakota, but I didn't know what town. I started calling North Dakota. The large cities, though there are not a lot of them. Anybody with his last name. I finally found the wife of one of George's cousins. She knew George's parents and gave me the number. I traced the name to a little town in North Dakota about ten miles from the Canadian border.

I sat by my phone thirty or forty minutes trying to decide if I should call. I picked up the phone, dialed the area code, put it back down. Pick it up, put it down. Over and over. I could open old wounds. They could hang up on me, and I knew that would destroy me. I called.

His mother answered. I said, "I'm not sure what this will do, but I just want you to know, my name is Jim Howarth from Tulsa, Oklahoma, and I was with your son when he died."

I waited and there was a pause. Then she started crying. I started crying. It turned out to be a wonderful experience. I was able to tell her some things the army couldn't.

I said, "I don't know if this is going to do anything, it's not going to bring George back, but I do want you to know he died instantly."

Long pause, sobbing. She said, "You don't know how long I've worried about that. Did he suffer? Did he lay out there a long time?"

I went to the Wall in November of '84, and I made an engraving of George's name, and I sent it to his parents. They have become friends of mine. We stay in touch.

Every one of those guys who died favored us with something, blessed us. That's the way I look at it, and I tell that to veterans I work with. That helps us live with it. I carry George with me every day.

GLOSSARY

Agent Orange: Toxic defoliant sprayed on vegetation to deny cover for the enemy.

Air burst: An explosive device, such as a grenade, artillery round, or mine, triggered or otherwise caused to detonate before touching ground in order to maximize the killing radius of shrapnel.

Air mobile: An infantry unit having its own squadron of helicopters or ready access to them.

AIT: Advanced individual training. For the Army infantry-man bound for Vietnam this was the second phase (nine weeks) of training.

AK47: Automatic assault rifle that was the standard weapon of Communist troops in Vietnam.

Alpha: The letter "A" in the military phonetic alphabet.

AO: Area of operations; Immediate area of responsibility for individual infantryman.

Ao-dai: Traditional dress of young Vietnamese women.

APC: Armored personnel carrier; armed track vehicle used to transport troops into battle.

ARVN: Army of the Republic of Vietnam; South Vietnamese government troops; a member of that army.

Attaboys: Verbal praise given U.S. pilots for a job well done.

Avenue of approach: Likely path assaulting troops might take on a defensive position.

B40: Shoulder-fired, rocket-propelled grenade launcher used by Communist troops.

Base camp: Headquarters of a battalion, brigade, or division.

Beaucoup: French for "many," pronounced by GIs "boocoo"; the second most-common adjective in the GI vocabulary in Vietnam.

Bird: Any aircraft, but usually a helicopter.

Bird dog: A light single-engined, propellered aircraft used to direct artillery fire or air support for ground troops.

Blooper: M-79 grenade launcher. Also called a chunker or thumper.

Blues: A reaction platoon; a member of that unit.

Body bags: Plastic and canvas bags in which American dead were taken from battle areas.

Booby trap: A concealed device, usually explosive, for the purpose of killing or maiming enemy soldiers. Used extensively by the Viet Cong against American personnel.

Bravo: The letter "B" in the military phonetic alphabet.

Bush: The jungle. Also called the field, the boonies, the boondocks.

Cammies: Camouflaged jungle combat fatigues, consisting of cap, blouse, and pants.

Cav: Cavalry.

C&C ship: Command and Control helicopter used by the commander at the battalion, brigade, or division level to direct battle action from above the contact.

Charlie: The letter *C* in the military phonetic alphabet; the enemy, as in Victor Charlie for Viet Cong, also known as Charles, Chuck, or Chas.

Cherry: Any new man just arrived to the bush.

Chicom: Weapons and ammunition manufactured by Chinese Communists.

Chieu Hoi: A government program to repatriate Viet Cong who voluntarily surrendered.

Chinook: Large transport helicopter.

Chopper: Helicopter.

CIB: Combat Infantry Badge. The award to men who have been fired upon in battle, an infantryman's mark of passage.

Claymore: Antipersonnel mine used in ambushes and defensive positions.

CO: Commanding officer.

Cobra: Helicopter gunship.

Company, the: Central Intelligence Agency

Connex: Large metal container used in Vietnam for transporting heavy equipment and on firebases for shelter as bunker hulls.

Contact: Firing on or being fired upon by the enemy.

Dap: A complicated, individualized rhythmic routine of slapping, pressing, and shaking hands in code used, largely by nonwhite soldiers, to demonstrate unity and trust.

Delta: The letter *D* in the military phonetic alphabet; the Mekong Delta.

DEROS: Date Eligible Return from Overseas; going home.

Deuce 'n' a half: Two-and-one-half-ton military transport truck.

Didi mau: Vietnamese for "get the hell out of here" (not literally).

Dog tags: Small metal identification plates worn around the neck by U.S. military personnel.

DTOC: Division Tactical Operations Center; also called TOC.

DMZ: Demilitarized Zone. Also called the D, the Z.

Dust-off: Helicopter conducting medical evacuation.

Echo: The letter *E* in the military phonetic alphabet.

E and E: Escape and evasion, which was the tactical mission of a U.S. combat soldier if captured or effectively cut off from his unit in battle.

Evac: Evacuation hospital or medical evacuation helicopter.

Extraction: Removal of troops from the field, usually by helicopter.

Firebase: Forward field artillery base.

Firefight: Small-arms battle.

FO: Forward observer.

Frag: Fragmentation grenade.

GI: Government Issue; a mostly affectionate term for a soldier of the U.S. Army or any equipment of that army.

Golf: The letter "G" in the military phonetic alphabet.

Gook: Derogatory slang for a Vietnamese person, especially a Viet Cong or NVA. Also, dink, slope, little man, Luke the Gook, Charlie, Charles, Chuck, Chas.

Green Beret: Member of the U.S. Special Forces.

Grunt: Army infantryman.

Gunship: Heavily armed helicopter to support infantry troops.

H.E.: High-explosive artillery round.

Hootch: Slang for any dwelling in Southeast Asia.

Huey: Army helicopter used primarily to transport troops on combat assaults.

Hump: To walk on patrol, usually heavily laden and heavily armed; to perform any difficult task.

I Corps: Northernmost military district of South Vietnam.

Incoming: Artillery rounds landing on a position.

In-country: In Vietnam.

Insertion: Placement of small helicopter-borne teams of Special Forces troops, Rangers, or scouts in the jungle.

Jody: Universal GI name for the guy back home who steals the GI's girl friend while he is away in Vietnam.

K: One kilometer; also called a klick.

Kabar: Combat knife.

KIA: Killed in action.

Kilo: The letter *K* in the military phonetic alphabet.

Kit Carson Scout: Former Viet Cong who had been repatriated and served as scout for American infantry units.

Lifer: A career soldier.

Little man: Slang for an enemy soldier, especially a Viet Cong.

LZ: Landing zone for helicopters. Usually a clearing in the jungle.

M-14: Heavy assault rifle used by American troops in the early years of the war.

M-16: Lightweight automatic assault rifle that became the standard American weapon in the war in Vietnam.

M-79: Grenade launcher, also called a blooper, chunker, thumper.

MACV: Military Assistance Command Vietnam, the headquarters of the American military command in-country.

Mamasan: A mature Vietnamese woman.

The Man: Black soldiers' slang for white authority.

Medevac: Slang for medical evacuation by a dust-off helicopter.

Montagnards: Highland tribesmen of Southeast Asia.

Nam: Vietnam.

NCO: A noncommissioned officer between the rank of corporal and sergeant major.

NDP: Night defensive position.

November: The letter ''N'' in the military phonetic alphabet.

Number ten: Very bad, as opposed to number one, which means very good.

NVA: The North Vietnamese Army or a member of that army.

OCS: Officer Candidate School.

Old man: Slang for commanding officer.

105: "One-oh-five," 105mm howitzer artillery gun.

Out: Out of Vietnam or out of the military service.

PF: Popular Forces, the local militia-like troops in the South Vietnamese countryside.

Point: Soldier breaking the trail, a unit's advance man in the line of march.

R&R: Rest and relaxation; a seven-day vacation offered to most American military personnel during their tour of duty in Vietnam, usually to one of several cities in Asia or the Pacific area.

Reaction platoon: Airmobile infantry unit on standby to come to the aid of units in contact. Also called Blues.

Rock 'n' roll: GI slang for firing a weapon on full automatic.

RPD: A light Communist-made machine gun.

RPG: Rocket-propelled grenade. See B40.

RTO: Radiotelephone operator; in the field the infantryman assigned to carry the unit radio and to maintain communications with support units.

Ruck: Infantryman's backpack. Also called a rucksack.

Sapper: An enemy soldier who infiltrates a position, usually armed with explosives.

Satchel charge: Explosives carried by a sapper, often strapped to his body.

Shake'n'Bake: A sergeant who earned his stripes by attending NCO school rather than by years of duty.

Short-time: Near the end of a tour of duty. Also called short.

SKS: A Russian-made semiautomatic rifle.

Slick: See Huey.

SP pack: Packet containing cigarettes and toiletries often given to infantrymen on resupply in the field.

Spec 4: Army person with the rank of E-4 between private first-class and sergeant.

Standdown: An infantry unit's return from the field to a firebase for rest and resupply.

Stars and Stripes: U.S. military newspaper.

Steel pot: Infantryman's helmet.

Tet: Vietnamese lunar New Year.

TL: Team leader.
TOC: Tactical Operations Center.
Tripwire: Fine metal wire placed along a trail or likely avenue of approach to trigger booby traps.
VC: Viet Cong.
Victor: The letter *V* in the military phonetic alphabet.
The Wall: The national Vietnam Veterans Memorial in Washington, D.C.
WIA: Wounded in action.
Willy pete: White phosphorus artillery round.
The World: Anywhere but Southeast Asia.

BIOGRAPHICAL SKETCHES

Stan Beesley is a teacher and writer. He and his family live in Pottawatomie County.

Rudolph Bridges lives with his family in Tulsa. He is a public school teacher and football coach.

Wilbert Brown and his family live in Tulsa where he is an ordained full-time Methodist minister.

Danny Bruner is a Creek full blood involved in tribal affairs. He is a lifetime resident of Broken Arrow, where he is a self-employed businessman.

David Carter, who lives with his family in Lexington, is editor of *The Oklahoma Veteran*. David is active in veterans groups and is working on the side of Agent Orange victims for recognition by the Veterans Administration and the U.S. government.

Danny Cruz is a veterans representative with the Oklahoma Job Service in Tulsa.

Max Dippel and his wife, Sue, and their two girls live in Weatherford. Max is head wrestling coach at the high school.

Terry Dyke is a financial consultant with Stifel Nicolaus. He also works as a pilot for American Airlines. He lives in Aydelotte with his wife and two sons.

Kathryn Fanning, widow of Major Hugh Fanning, lives in Oklahoma City, where she is a writer and a teacher. Their three children are now grown.

Bob Ford and his family live in Okeene, where he is president of Okeene Mills. He is active in civic organizations.

Marguerite Giroux is head of nursing at the Veterans Administration Hospital in Oklahoma City. She retired as a colonel from the U.S. Army, and she is near retirement from civilian nursing.

Mark Hatfield helps his brother and father on the family farm near Coweta. Mark is a postal routeman. He and his wife have three children.

Willie Homer teaches in the Shawnee public schools.

Jim Howarth and his family live in Tulsa. He is codirector of the Tulsa Vet Center.

Morris James retired from the army in 1982. He now works in sales in the Shawnee area. He and his wife, Jean Ann, have a daughter and a son.

Lee and Betsy Keyes, who met through letters to each other while Lee was in Vietnam, have three children and live with them in Tulsa.

Robert Kirk is professor of education at Southwestern State University. He is a deacon of the First Baptist Church in Weatherford, where he and his family live.

Gary LaBass is counselor at Owasso High School. Gary and his wife live in Owasso with their two children.

J.D. Maples and his family live in Broken Arrow. J.D. is a teacher and financial consultant.

David Mead is a counselor at the Tulsa Vet Center. He and his family live in Tulsa.

Greg Motto is director of physical plant operations at the University of Tulsa. He is a professional artist. He and his family make their home in Claremore.

Bill Poffenberger lives with his family in Tulsa. Bill is a postal worker.

David Price is a painter. He and his wife, Georgann, live in Hominy.

Stephen Redman lives in Sapulpa, where he is active in the Disabled American Veterans chapter.

David Samples and his family built a country home near Porter. He is self-employed. David is a poet and writer.

Gary Sherrer is a rancher in Snow, where he lives with his wife and two daughters.

Don Sloat was one of eight men from Coweta killed in Vietnam. The letters for "Love, Son" were submitted by his mother, Mrs. Evelyn Sloat.

Norman Summers is a social psychologist specializing in drug and alcohol rehabilitation. He is active in the Vietnam Veterans of Oklahoma. He and his wife and two children live in Sallisaw.

Billy Walkabout is recognized as one of the most highly decorated Americans of the Vietnam War. A Cherokee full blood, Billy is active in intertribal affairs. A movie on his life story has been proposed. He lives in Oklahoma City with his wife, Joy, and their children.

Jack Welsh is the head of endocrinology at the University of Oklahoma Health Sciences Center in Oklahoma City. Among his many duties is working with Vietnamese doctors who have come to America since the fall of Saigon.

Les Weston works for the Williams Companies of Tulsa. He is president of the Northeast Chapter of the Vietnam Veterans of Oklahoma. He and his family live in Tulsa.

Melvin Wren lives near Bethel with his family. He is a retired army sergeant major. He is Disabled American Veterans representative for Pottawatomie County.

Jim Yearout is a veterans representative for the Oklahoma Job Service. He and his family live in Harrah.

Index